KENSINGTON
PAST

TO OUR FAMILIES

Acknowledgements

In writing this book we are indebted to the research of those local historians who have gone before us and who provided the source materials from which we worked. We wish to thank all those who have so generously donated paintings and photographs to the Kensington and Chelsea Libraries and Arts Service, many of which we have used in this book. We have been greatly assisted by the staff of the Local Studies department, in particular Kathryn McCord.

We would also like to thank our families for their forbearance and encouragement and the practical assistance of Philip Denny in checking the index.

Lastly, but not least, we would like to thank our publisher and editor, John Richardson, for his disciplined but sensitive handling of the manuscript.

The Illustrations

With the exception of those listed below, all the illustrations are reproduced by kind permission of the Royal Borough of Kensington and Chelsea Libraries and Arts Service.
Barbara Denny: *9, 39, 44, 60, 69, 77, 96, 98, 114, 115, 146, 152, 159, 171*
Historical Publications: *10, 12, 24, 26, 83, 85, 141, 147, 165, 178*
Peter Jackson Collection: *110, 111*

First published 1998
by Historical Publications Ltd
32 Ellington Street, London N7 8PL
(Tel: 0171-607 1628)

ISBN 0 948667 50 8
British Library Cataloguing-in-Publication Data
A catalogue record for this book is available from the British Library.

Typeset in Palatino by Historical Publications Ltd
Reproduction by G & J Graphics, London EC2
Printed in Zaragoza, Spain by Edelvives.

KENSINGTON PAST

Barbara Denny
Carolyn Starren

HISTORICAL PUBLICATIONS

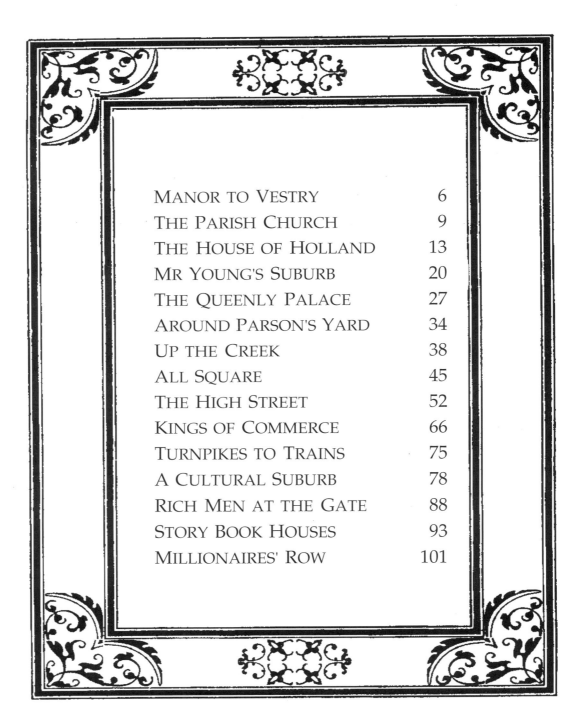

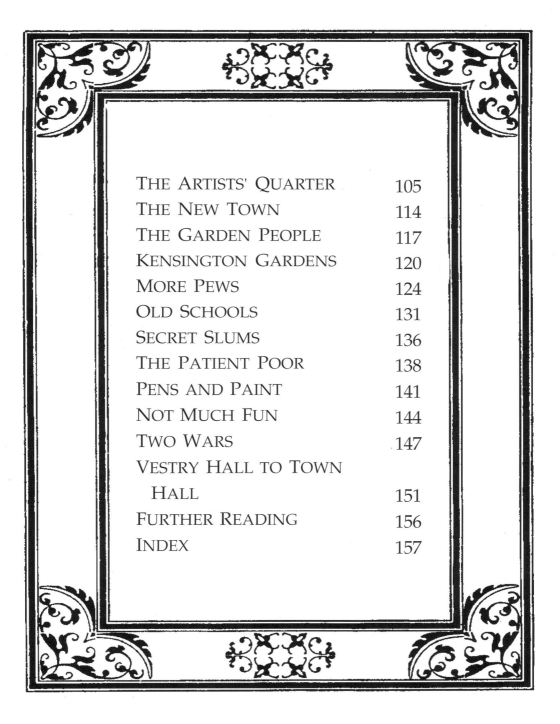

1. *Outside St Mary Abbots church in Kensington High Street in 1869, before the present church was built.*
In earlier days, this was at the heart of local government.

Manor to Vestry

BEGINNINGS

An archaeological dig on the site of St Mary Abbots Hospital in Marloes Road in recent years has found prehistoric and Roman remains – Iron Age pottery, post holes and pits sealed under a layer of alluvium. Until then the only hint of a Roman presence in Kensington was on the northern highway to Oxford, now Holland Park Avenue.

The name of Kensington is Saxon. It is *Chenesitun* in Domesday Book, probably derived from the 'tun' of Cynesige's people, and the spellings have ranged from that to Kinsentona or Keynsington. It is thought that the first settlement was around the site of St Mary Abbots church which thereafter was the heart of the village.

At the time of the Conquest the manor was given

The first evidence of a priest in Kensington is in Domesday Book where he is noted as holding about 15 acres.

In medieval times and up to the seventeenth century local affairs were the responsibility of the manors and the parish vestry meetings. The former dealt with land transactions, the maintenance of streams and highways, the appointment of some local officers, and the latter dealt with charitable bequests, the destitute and church matters. But gradually the manor lost its influence in parish affairs, especially after the Poor Law Act of 1601 which placed the responsibility for poor relief squarely on the parish whose business was conducted in the Vestry Room of the church, under the chairmanship of the vicar. As more and more responsibilities were given to the parish the 'Vestry' came to be the recognised local authority. This pertained in Kensington until the end of the nineteenth century, when London vestries were abolished and merged into larger boroughs.

The Vestry of Kensington had jurisdiction over the whole of Kensington and thus over not only Abbots Manor, but the manors of Earls Court, West Town (on the Hammersmith border) and the northern manor of Notting Barns.

The Vestry or Town meeting usually took place once a year, with ratepayers in the village entitled to attend, to choose officers such as the Constable, Surveyor of Highways and an Overseer of the Poor. These posts were unpaid, generally allocated by rote and were avoided if possible. The only paid servant was the Vestry Clerk, who was appointed for life.

In the seventeenth century Kensington was a quiet village known to travellers on the two main roads westward out of London. It rose to prominence, and serious development began, with the purchase of Nottingham House by William and Mary in 1689, at which time the newly named Kensington Palace became the principal residence of the monarch. Inevitably, despite its nearness to the West End, Kensington became popular with the Court and the tradesmen who supplied the royal household. George III deserted the Palace but by the beginning of the nineteenth century royal occupants once again helped to renew the prestige of the area. By 1821 the population of Kensington was 13,428, and in 1851, when it had reached 44,053, a Vestry Hall was built in the High Street, meetings before having been held in a room off the church. This original Vestry Hall (now the Melli Bank) is the only substantial remnant of the Victorian High Street. In its early days handsome railings and other ornamentation fronted it, which gave rise to accusations of extravagance on the part of the vestrymen. 'The parish has been

to Geoffrey, Bishop of Coutances who in turn passed it to Aubrey de Vere in 1093. The de Veres, who later became the Earls of Oxford, were to retain the manor, which covered about 3½ square miles, for the next 500 years. However, Godfrey de Vere gave a small area around the old chapel of St Mary to the Abbey of Abingdon in 1100 as thanks for their care of his son during a serious illness. This 270-acre gift became known as the Abbots Manor and its church as St Mary Abbots.

encumbered with a millstone board of nothing-ness', wrote one ratepayer in the *Kensington Gazette* in 1854. Another, complaining about the poor street lighting, said that this would have been remedied 'had the agitation been for extra gold lace on the Beadle's uniform or a peacock to strut in the courtyard.'

By that time staff had increased considerably and in 1867 the *Kensington Directory* gives the name of the Vestry Clerk as Reuben Green and the parish Beadle had the apt name of Mr S. Pummell. In addition there was a Sanitary Inspector and an Inspector of Nuisances. The Vestry had 120 elected members, although a meeting of ratepayers com-plained that the seats were becoming hereditary. Accusations of extravagance continued and the clerks were said 'to be found scribbling on paper to amuse themselves', and the Borough Engineer 'not doing much except ride about'. He was receiving a salary of £300 a year and asking for £50 for a trap.

Despite its many aristocratic residents over the years, Kensington, like many London areas, had a good number of slum areas with almost non-existent sanitary arrangements. Night soil men emptied cesspits from houses without sewer con-nections. In 1851 Kensington obtained an Im-provement Act which allowed them to repair old footways and co-ordinate the lighting of the streets.

In 1900 the old Vestry of St Mary Abbots, under the reorganisation of London government, became the Borough of Kensington, though in 1901 by the wish of Queen Victoria, who was born in Kensing-ton Palace, it was given a Royal Charter. At the same time, with boundary adjustment, the Palace was placed officially in Kensington (it was pre-viously in the parish of St John and St Margaret, Westminster).

2. Kensington Vestry Hall in the High Street, in 1852. Today this is the Melli Bank.

The Parish Church

The first evidence of the existence of a parish priest in Kensington is in the Domesday Book where he is accounted as holding about fifteen acres of land. The chapel he served would have been part of the manorial estate held by Aubrey de Vere as the gift of William after the Conquest. It was Aubrey's son Godfrey, who on his death bed bequeathed the land and church to the Benedictine Abbey of St Mary of Abingdon in Berkshire.

It was not until the thirteenth century that the Abbot established a church in Kensington as an independent parish with an endowment for a vicar. The first to be recorded by name was Nicholas who appeared on the Patent Roll of Henry III in 1242. There is no archaeological evidence of a medieval building although records exist of a valuation of £17. 6s. 8d. in 1219 and bequests appear in various wills between then and the sixteenth century. It is known that the church consisted of a nave, chancel and a tower about 50 feet high with a little spire and a clock, presented by Sir William Williamson.

The tower was all that was to remain after the Bishop gave permission in 1683 for the church to be rebuilt as it was then too small to house the growing congregation. By the time the work began, King William and Queen Mary were living at Kensington Palace and gave £300 towards the cost; Princess Anne gave £100.

The new church was described as being 'very large and spacious, built of brick and paved handsomely with Purbeck stone.' However, due to unstable foundations, it had to be closed in 1704 for repairs and services were held in the private chapel of Holland House at the invitation of the Countess of Warwick. Eventually, the medieval building was declared unsafe and replaced in 1772 with a red brick one.

As the population grew steadily in the nineteenth century, fourteen ecclesiastical districts were created in Kensington to take the strain off the parish church. The Bishop of London, Charles Blomfield, had already declared St Mary Abbots to be the ugliest church in his diocese and soon the description 'most dangerous' could have been added, as its walls were bulging and there was dry rot in the beams.

After an inspection by two architects it was declared unsafe in 1866 and the Vicar, Archdeacon Sinclair, decided that a new church should be built 'on a scale proportionate to the opulence and importance of a great Metropolitan parish.'

3. *The west view of St Mary Abbots church in 1822.*

DEMOLITION

Demolition did not actually begin until 1869, when *The Kensington News* reported that the clock and organ had been removed as well as the Church-warden's pew which had been 'guarded by a grim lion and full bodied unicorn.' The pulpit, which had already suffered 'barbarous treatment' by being painted over, was to be installed in the new church. The day before the bells were taken down, the anniversary of Queen Victoria's Coronation, the Kensington bell ringers 'rang out merry peals' which had been preceded two days earlier by the Cumberland Society's peal of over five thousand changes in three hours.

The architect chosen to design the new church was George Gilbert Scott, who was already busy on the Albert Memorial. The new building was consecrated in 1872 although the tower was not completed until 1879. Dr John Merriman, an enthusiastic amateur photographer, kept a fascinating pictorial record of the progress of the demolition from the top windows of his house in Kensington Square. The spire, said to be the highest in London and the sixth highest in England, was originally recorded as 278 feet but in more recent times is said to be 250

4. The interior of the new St Mary Abbots Church.

feet, plus a 14-foot vane. The top stone of the spire was laid by the vicar, the Rev Edward Carr Glyn. With twelve parishioners and two churchwardens, one being Jubal Webb the cheesemonger, and a correspondent of *The Times*, he climbed the scaffolding and held a service over 200 feet above the crowds below. It was a blustery day and *The Times* reported that the scaffolding was swaying slightly in the wind as the Vicar laid the cap stone in position, using a silver trowel. The Rev. Glyn, vicar from 1879 to 1897 when he was appointed Bishop of Peterborough, married a granddaughter of Queen Victoria.

The spire houses a peal of ten bells on which the clock chimes the hours and quarters, although there is no visible clock face because it was thought it might spoil the look of the spire. Of the older bells, some had already been recast in 1772 and others were recast in 1879 at the same time as two new bells were added. The larger of these bears the inscription 'those evening bells how many a tale their music tells' and the smaller, 'Warn, Rejoice, Mourn.' Among the other inscriptions is the curiously pagan 'the ringers' art our grateful notes prolong, Apollo listens and approves the song.' The ringers' art is regularly heard from the belfry and on celebratory and mourning occasions, including the funeral of Princess Diana.

The arcaded cloister from Kensington High Street to the south door was added in 1889-93, designed by John Oldred Scott, son of Sir George Gilbert Scott.

5. St Mary Abbots church after 1879, when the spire had been completed.

6. The scene at St Mary Abbots after an incendiary raid on 14 March, 1944.

In March 1944 the church was hit by an incendiary bomb and the nave roof totally destroyed. The fact that no greater damage was done was due in no small measure to the efforts of voluntary fire watchers. The story is told that one of them sat at the organ as hoses played on the burning roof, playing hymns and the National Anthem to keep the cascading water out of the pipes. Until rebuilding could begin after the war, services were held under a temporary canopy, the new wooden nave designed by Romilly Craze being installed in 1955. Most of the St Mary Abbots plate is now housed at the Victoria & Albert Museum. It includes an Elizabethan silver gilt cup, a decorated silver flagon of 1619 and a silver alms dish given to the parish by Elizabeth Knightly, daughter of John Hampden and cousin of Oliver Cromwell.

With its proximity to Kensington Palace it is not surprising that the congregation has often included members of the royal family. In our times among the most faithful was the Princess Alice, Countess of Athlone who lived to the great age of 98.

Much of what is still known about the monuments inside the church and outside in the burial ground is the result of devoted work undertaken by the late J. P. Hill, whose scholarly paper appeared in the church's newsletter some years ago. He concluded that very few if any of the monuments are in their original positions for the whole lay-out of the site was altered when the old church was demolished. The workmen removed the inscribed slabs that covered the burial vaults in the chancel, nave and aisles and placed them in the churchyard, 'an act which many of us regard as vandalism', although most of them were eventually replaced in the new building. Among the most interesting are the seated figure in white marble, the monument to the 7th Earl of Warwick, and the kneeling angel in the Resurrection Chapel carved by Princess Louise in memory of her brothers the Dukes of Edinburgh and Albany.

7. The St Mary Abbots church plate, now in the V & A.

8. The Earl of Warwick's tomb in St Mary Abbots.

MYSTERY MONUMENTS

Without doubt the most interesting memorial in the church – and the only relic of its medieval past – is that to Henry Dawson of Newcastle, a member of Cromwell's 'Barebones' parliament, who died in 1635. How a Roundhead came to be buried in an Anglican Church is a story researched to great reward by Mr A. Jabez Smith, of the Kensington Society. The Society together with the Society of Antiquities of Newcastle-upon-Tyne and English Heritage has been responsible for rescuing the marble memorial from its banishment.

Gilbert Scott apparently did not consider it of more than historic value and unsuitable in his Gothic edifice. Over a century of wind and weather had reduced it to a very dilapidated condition when efforts were made to restore it and also to find out more of its story. The vicar of St Mary Abbots at the time of the Civil War was Thomas Hodges who was highly regarded by the Commonwealth Parliament. It is possible that 'a Church of Christ' in London, to whom Dawson left a bequest of 22 shillings as a token in his will, may have been that at Kensington, although all his other connections are with Newcastle. The plaque, now restored and fixed to the inside wall of the church, contains much biographical detail.

Another recent restoration was carried out by the Soane Monuments Trust. This was of the 'mystery' sarcophagus of Elizabeth Johnstone who was only 23 when she died in 1784 'to the tears and bitterness of heart of her disconsolate friends.' Some zealous modern detective work revealed that the 'bath shaped' tomb which stands beneath a large chestnut tree in the churchyard a few yards from the west front, had been designed by the famous architect, Sir John Soane, and had been commissioned by the Earl of Bellamont. The mystery was, what connection did the Earl have with a young lady described as 'the eldest daughter of Mr Robert Johnstone, gentleman of Brompton'?

The appeal for funds to pay for its restoration very soon elicited a response from a descendant of Elizabeth Johnstone which clarified the mystery. A family portrait exists of a pretty young woman with a little boy of about three years old on her lap. From his hand dangles a miniature of a handsome man – his father, the Rt. Hon Charles Coote, Baron Conooly and Earl of Bellamont.

Although commended in his time for his comeliness and courage, Lord Bellamont was also known as 'the Hibernian seducer', although it seems that his relationship with the unfortunate Elizabeth was happy while it lasted. There was a romantic but bigamous marriage and the birth of a boy in 1780 when the couple were in England, but when he returned to Ireland, after they had spent some time travelling abroad, Elizabeth insisted on accompanying him and there the story ends. It is assumed that she returned to England where she died and her penitent betrayer was moved to pay a tribute to her 'gentle pride and tenderness her constancy and truth.' The little boy was taken into the Earl's family until his adulthood when no more is known of him.

Among other monuments are those to Royal Physicians, David Middleton (d.1785), Sergeant Surgeon to the King and Surgeon General to the Army, and Richard Warren (d.1797). Humbler servants who have their memorials are the coachman, William Mason, who after serving the royal family for 48 years, died in 1838, and several domestics of the Duke of Sussex, brother to George IV. The royal family were not alone in paying tribute to their employees. Mary Stephens, who died in 1820, aged 72, having served 44 years with one family, is described as 'an affectionate and faithful and attached friend.' Another memorial is dedicated to an Indian, with the improbable name of George Mortlake, who served William Townshend and his family for more than 50 years and died in 1830 at the age of 63.

The House of Holland

9. Henry Rich (1590-1649), 1st Earl of Holland.

10. South front of Holland House; watercolour by John Buckler, 1812.

Remarkably, a fragment of old Holland House remains, surrounded by parkland and gardens. Over four centuries it has seen Civil War, political intrigue, changes of ownership and financial crises.

In 1599, Sir Walter Cope, described as a 'gentleman of rare and excellent parts' and very rich, bought the freehold of the four manors that make up today's Kensington. It was a wise investment for a man who had wide trade interests, a grand house in the Strand and who was to become a favourite at the Court of James I. But it was the western area of the manor known as West Town, which really took his fancy and here he decided to build a house so grand that it would soon be known as Cope's Castle.

Additional wings, designed by John Thorpe, would be added later to the splendid Jacobean mansion he had constructed, where entertainment was lavish as might be expected when the guests often included royalty.

But Cope was not to enjoy his new home for long and was still planning new additions when he died in 1614, leaving the house and its surrounding parkland to his wife and thereafter to his daughter

11. *The Journal Room at Holland House in 1886.*

Isabel, who came into possession when her mother remarried. Isabel herself had made a very good marriage, which was as well for despite his life-style, or perhaps because of it, Sir Walter had died heavily in debt. Her young husband, Sir Henry Rich, second son of the Earl of Warwick was the epitome of a nobleman, tall, good-looking and wealthy and within two years of their marriage he had been created Baron Kensington and Earl of Holland. He willingly took over the improvements of what until then had been Kensington House, giving it his new name of Holland, which came from his property in Lincolnshire. He was also a royal favourite. In 1624 he had been an emissary in the arrangements for the marriage of Prince Charles and the Princess Henrietta Maria who thereafter showed fondness towards him.

But political deviance was to prove his undoing. Switching from side to side before and during the Civil War he eventually finished on the losing side, and as a result, Rich's handsome head, wearing a smart lace cap, was severed from his body outside Westminster Hall on 9 March 1649. His body was interred at St Mary Abbots and his ghost, carrying his head under his arm, was believed to haunt the Gilt Room of Holland House – created in happier times to celebrate the wedding of Charles and Henrietta Maria – leaving three drops of blood.

Holland House was commandeered by the Cromwellian forces as headquarters for Colonel Fairfax and it was on the great 19-acre meadow in front of the house that Cromwell and Ireton are said to have discussed strategy because Ireton's deafness made it necessary to shout.

The occupation was short and Henry Rich's widow was soon allowed to return, whereon she resumed her social life and building improvements continued. Her son, who eventually inherited the house and the Warwick earldom, died in 1675. It was his grandson, who became the 4th Earl of Holland when he was only four years old, and whose widowed mother, Charlotte, married Joseph Addison in 1713.

During her widowhood Charlotte had often let Holland House, one tenant being, it is believed, William Penn the founder of Pennsylvania. Although Addison had courted Charlotte for some years while he had been tutor to her little son the eventual marriage was not a happy one, possibly because he was already suffering from asthma and dropsy.

Addison had done his best to foster the 'young lord' through his early years although he was apparently a difficult boy. It was to be of no great importance, for Edward Henry died when he was in his early twenties. He stands in marble effigy in St Mary Abbots Church not looking at all 'vicious or depraved' as one biographer has described him. His death broke the direct line of succession, the house and 200-acre estate passing to distant relatives, the Edwardes family, through the marriage of Elizabeth, grand daughter of the beheaded Earl, but they did not live there long.

By 1726 the property was leased to the notorious Henry Fox, the Whig Paymaster General who was described at one time as a public defaulter of unaccountable millions. Whatever his faults may have been, Fox was undoubtedly the saviour of the old house, which was in a poor state of repair. When Fox eventually succeeded in his efforts to acquire a peerage in 1763, he took his title from Holland House, becoming the first Baron Holland, and acquired the freehold in 1768.

Henry Fox's father, Sir Stephen Fox, had also made a fortune from his position as Paymaster General of the Forces at the time of the Restoration but had also been a prime mover in the foundation of Chelsea Hospital. His elder son, of the same name, also did well in a political career and was created Earl of Ilchester in 1756, his descendant becoming the owner of Holland House just over a century later.

Although Henry Fox's public life seems to have been somewhat dubious his family life was unblemished. He proved a faithful and devoted husband to Lady Caroline Lennox, daughter of the Duke of Richmond, with whom he eloped in 1744.

It was during their lives that the foundations were laid of the gardens for which the house was to become famous. He was great admirer of the new fashion of landscape gardening and invited William Kent, Charles Hamilton and Peter Collinson to work on the grounds. A great variety of rare specimens, especially American trees, were planted, many from his father-in-law's estate at Goodwood.

In a letter to Collinson, Henry Fox said he was trying to grow Cypresses, Scarlet Oaks and Chestnuts from seed and 'I need a bushel or more'. Lady Caroline also had 'a thousand questions to ask about flowers'.

They had three sons, Stephen, a second who died in infancy, and the third who was the famous Charles James. Delicate and precocious, Charles was terribly spoilt by parents who called him 'Mr Thumb'. Even at Eton he was allocated a private tutor. In adulthood he was clever and popular and became one of the most famous characters of his age, statesman, Leader of the Opposition and Foreign Secretary, despite the fact that his father had to buy him his first seat in Parliament. He drank, gambled, owned thirty racehorses, tested his public popularity to extremes and ran heavily

12. *Rogers' Seat and the Inigo Jones gateway at Holland House.*

into debt. He was unmarried but he was the heir apparent to the title since his brother Stephen was ailing and childless. Then, in 1773/4, Stephen's wife had a son, Lord Holland and his wife died within a few weeks of each other and Stephen died in November of the same year. The 3rd Baron Holland was therefore a baby of a year old. He and his mother left Holland House to live in the country and the mansion that had been the scene of so much glittering entertainment was let out to tenants.

Surprisingly, Charles James Fox took to the 'young one' as he called him. The little boy was sent to Eton when he was only seven and remained there 'without disgrace or distinction' until he went to Oxford. He travelled widely in Europe and it was during these travels that he met and fell in love with Elizabeth Webster, who with him would reign over the most famous period in Holland House's history. Elizabeth, the victim of an early arranged marriage to a man many times her age, was 23 but had already five children by him. Holland was two years younger. He was not in the least handsome, she wrote 'but still quite delightful'. They became constant companions and she was expecting his child when her marriage ended in divorce in 1797.

Despite the social stigma of such a sensational divorce, Elizabeth became one of the leading hostesses of the times and Holland House was a centre of political and social life. Much of Elizabeth's fortune, inherited from her father, had been seized by her husband on their divorce but when he committed suicide in the midst of gambling debts in 1800 she regained most of it, although she never recovered her children by him.

Lady Holland's Salon was legendary. Here moved many of the famous names of the early nineteenth century; all are recorded in her 'Dinner Books'. She was domineering and sharp tongued – many anecdotes confirm this – but she must also have had charm because even the guests she scolded always came back for more. She was intelligent, if not highly educated and an inveterate collector. The Journal Room at Holland House was literally stuffed with her acquisitions on their journeys, cases of butterflies and insects, collections of minerals, stuffed birds and animals – ninety-six boxes of them – and endless 'curios'. She also made improvements to the garden and it was during her time that the Dutch Garden was laid out and the first dahlias grown, the seed having been sent over from Spain. Facing the dahlias was Rogers' Seat, named after the poet/banker Samuel Rogers.

As a prominent Whig, Lord Holland was expected to become Foreign Secretary. However the Cabinet decided that they could not tolerate a man whose wife opened his letters and Sir John Russell was sent to convey the bad news. This encouraged Lord Holland to open his house to foreign liberals and for a time Holland House became a centre of English Napoleonism. A bust of Napoleon by Canova was erected on a pedestal in the Dutch Garden and presents were sent to him in exile on St Helena, including jars of Lady Holland's special plum jam. In his will Napoleon left her a snuffbox.

Lord Holland died on 22 October 1840 and Lady Holland wrote in her Dinner Book 'This wretched day closes all the happiness, refinement and hospitality within the walls of Holland House'.

She survived her husband for five years living mainly in London at Great Stanhope Street, only visiting Holland House occasionally or sometimes staying with her sister-in-law, Caroline Fox, nearby at Little Holland House. Her son, Henry, the 4th and last Lord Holland, spent much time abroad, and was as worried over the state of his inheritance as he was that his mother might dispose of it. From 1822 the estate had slowly started to be broken up as land was leased off for building to meet the costs, not only of maintenance but also the Hollands' lavish life style. When Henry and his wife Lady Mary Augusta inherited the house, this did not diminish for it was she who had the Garden Ballroom and the Orangery built 1847/50 with the terrace walk to them. Today the Ballroom is the Belvedere Restaurant and the Orangery is used as an art venue. Other alterations included decorations by the young G. F. Watts.

13. *Lady Mary Augusta, who died in 1889.*

The Hollands were childless although they adopted a baby girl in 1851, a French child who later became the Princess Liechtenstein. In 1873, faced with enormous financial difficulties and rejecting such drastic action as selling off the whole estate for building, she decided to anticipate its inheritance by a distant relative, the 5th Earl of Ilchester, by making it over to him in her lifetime in return for an annuity. This was certainly the salvation of the building which was then extensively repaired, and in the remaining seventy years during the occupancy of the Ilchesters, returned to much of its old glory. It is difficult now to imagine the lavish décor of this great old mansion with its tiled hall, elaborate carved grand staircase, rich silk and velvet furnishings, carved and painted ceilings, statues and busts, packed with fine furniture, glass and silver, paintings and a magnificently stocked library. The last grand occasion in July 1939 was attended by George VI and Queen Elizabeth and was described in later years by a 16-year-old parlour maid. 'We saw the Earl lead the Queen on the floor with the King leading the Countess. There were flowers everywhere, the house was floodlit outside and a band was playing in the Orangery. The smell of jasmine filled the air, the scene was unforgettable'.

Just over a year later, during the night of 27/28 September, 1940, incendiary bombs rained down upon the house during the Blitz. At 6am the 6th

14. The 5th Earl of Ilchester, by Spy.

left of the building described in 1925 as 'the finest remaining example of the country house in London...'

In 1952 the grounds were opened to the public. These were managed by Frederick Hilliard of the LCC and then GLC, who kept them as a 'private estate' open to the public, without 'muncipalising' them. In 1978 a Friends group was formed to encourage the continuation of Hilliard's work.

Eventually, the East Wing was restored as part of the King George VI Memorial Youth Hostel, together with the buildings designed by Hugh Casson and Neville Conder – again not without considerable public debate and controversy.

But there are still two cedars planted by Henry Fox on the north lawn and if the woodland trees are not those planted by gardeners of long ago they at least grew from the seeds of those trees. Likewise wild flowers have seeded themselves since the days when Lady Sarah Lennox posed as a country wench to catch the eye of the Prince of Wales, the future George III in 1759.

The Nicholas Stone pier gates were constructed in 1629 for the south front of the house but moved to the East Wing when that became the main entrance. They were approached by steps above a water lily pool with a fountain. Today they form the main entrance to the opera stage on the south front. The Ice House, recovered and restored in recent times as a small art gallery, dates from the 1770s, later becoming a dairy, just as the Garden Ballroom created by the last Lady Holland was once a stable granary. The Orangery once contained rows of marble pedestals topped with busts of friends of the Hollands.

In the 1960s the GLC revived the tradition of open-air theatre here. This was later taken over by the Royal Borough's Libraries and Arts Service and each June a huge canopy rises in front of the south facade of the old house heralding the start of the Holland Park opera season.

The Green Lane is now Abbotsbury Road. The old grassy pathway edged with trees was a favourite spot of Charles Fox and he came for a final visit just before his death. Nightingale Lane, now Ilchester Place, is where Lady Diana Rich is said by John Aubrey to have met her own apparition 'as in a looking glass' and died a month later of small-pox. When the last Lord Holland closed this right of way, which also ran in front of the house, he was obliged to give the public Holland Walk from the High Street to Holland Park Avenue.

The Kyoto Garden created in recent years as a collaborative effort between the Royal Borough and the Kyoto Chamber of Commerce is not an innovation but a restoration of the Japanese garden laid out by the Earl of Ilchester in 1902.

Earl came up from his country house in Dorset and watched the melancholy sight of firemen damping down the charred remains.

Happily, most of its more valuable contents had been removed before the outbreak of war but there was still much remaining, including the contents of the huge library and as much of this as possible was salvaged.

At the end of the war, the House and grounds were offered to the London County Council but it was to be another seven years before this happened. Deterioration took place while arguments raged as to what should be done with what was

15. *A garden party at Holland House, c1872.*

16. *The Orangery at Holland House in 1886.*

Mr Young's Suburb

Kensington Square, lying behind the shops and offices of the High Street, has retained enough of its Georgian charm to deserve the description it was given soon after its creation when Daniel Defoe, in 1705, considered that Kensington centred on this 'noble Square full of good houses'.

It undoubtedly owed its later reputation to the presence of the Court in Kensington, but that was not the reason for its construction. It was the dream of Thomas Young, a woodcarver in the tradition of Grinling Gibbons, to produce a beautiful residential square in the fields near the old parish church of St Mary Abbots.

Thomas Young is believed to have been born in Devon and was apprenticed to a joiner and woodcarver, being admitted as a freeman of the Joiners' Company in 1670 when he was about twenty. Very soon after this he was among the woodcarvers employed by Wren, rebuilding the City churches. From this one can surmise that he was artistic, a craftsman rather than a business man.

Although he worked for speculators, Kensington Square was his first venture on his own ac-

17. Nos. 11 and 12 Kensington Square. Used as part of John Gardnor's Drawing Academy in the 1760s.

count, undertaken in 1685, and this may explain his subsequent financial difficulties. His acquisition of fourteen acres of land and a 'mansion house', which was soon demolished, was heavily mortgaged. Obviously he could not carry out so great an undertaking by himself and offered most of the building sites to others for development, hoping 'to complete the Square with all convenience possible'. About twenty builders responded, many of whom were as equally skilled craftsmen as himself and he reserved only six sites for his own use, together with a plot on the south-west side to make a Spring Garden and Bowling Green. Here he built the twelve-roomed Bowling Green House where he dwelt with his wife and children, 'a substantial three-storey villa richly painted, wainscoted and adorned' which was also to provide a place for entertainment, eating and drinking. It was surrounded by a garden and Young considered it would be not only an attraction for the inhabitants of the Square but provide him and his family with a living.

He was heavily in debt and his financial backer, Thomas Sutton, an 'Indian Gown Seller' of the Strand, was pressing for some return. So in 1686 Young sold off land on the west side which was still undeveloped, as well as the freehold of a number of house sites, but he continued to borrow more money for building purposes.

Within six months however he was arrested for debt and lodged in the King's Bench Prison. While there he was persuaded by Sutton 'pretending great love and kindness' to hand over the equity of redemption on the mortgages to prevent his other creditors seizing it and leaving him to 'perish in prison and his family to come to ruin'. This gave Sutton not only the freehold of those parts of the Square he already held under mortgage but also the Bowling Green House and Spring Garden.

Young returned to work at Chatsworth from 1688 to 1691 but by the end of that year found himself back in 'close prison in the Fleet' where he remained for almost ten years despite trying to raise a loan to pay Sutton. Eventually Young brought a case against Sutton in Chancery. High on his list of complaints was the treatment of his bowling green and garden which he said Sutton had 'quite digged up'.

During these years of misfortune others were filling the Square with the houses which were to impress Defoe and others, such as Thomas Bowack, who thought it the most beautiful part of Kensington. Those who took building sites included other Wren workmen and although the Square gives an impression of uniformity the houses are very different, both inside and out, according to the fancies of their owners. Those who are lucky enough to have seen inside them know they still contain some magnificent staircases, interesting chimney pieces and beautiful plasterwork. One long-time resident, Arthur, Lord Ponsonby of Shulbrede, wrote a history of the Square and its residents.

The Ponsonby family itself provided interesting material. Arthur Ponsonby moved into no. 17 when he married the daughter of the composer Hubert Parry, in 1886. His grandson, the Hon. Thomas Ponsonby, later became a Labour councillor and alderman and as Lord Ponsonby moved into central government.

THE CARRIAGE FOLK

The removal of the Court of King William and Queen Mary from Whitehall to Nottingham House in Kensington ensured the Square's success. Almost every house built was occupied by 1696, although with more tenants and lodgers than long-term residents. For four reigns, until the death of George II in 1760, the Square became the home of persons of quality, ambassadors, gentry and clergy. Thomas Faulkner recorded 'At one time upwards of 40 carriages were kept in and about the neighbourhood'. But the royal residents had a number of homes – Whitehall, St James, Hampton Court, Kew and Windsor – and moved among them with amazing frequency. George I favoured Kensington for the midsummer months, but there was little room for his retinue, many of whom found lodgings in the Square. Courtiers included Adam Lisney, Groom of the Bedchamber to William III who leased no. 5 for three years from 1695, at £20 a year, but actually remained in possession for nearly forty, until 1733. During that time his house was also used by several other royal servants such as the poet, Sir Fleetwood Sheppard, Usher of the Black Rod.

Another was the Lord Chamberlain, Robert Spencer, second Earl of Sunderland, who is described by the *Dictionary of National Biography* as the 'craftiest, most rapacious and most unscrupulous politician of his age.' Adam Lisney moved a few doors to no. 8 at the end of his life, dying there in 1741, aged over ninety. Another resident at no. 8 was a clergyman of ill repute, the son of the Archbishop of York. He was Dr Thomas Lamplugh a 'little sneaking, stingy, self-interested fellow who hindered his father from good works.' The house was demolished in 1901 to build Abbots Court flats.

Many of the early residents were those who had performed good service to the Crown, such as John, Baron Cutts of Gowran. He served under William of Orange at the Battle of Buda and played a prominent part in the Irish campaign for which he received an Irish barony in 1690. He was the

first occupant of no. 23 from 1696-1702 during which time his private secretary was Richard Steele.

It was natural that William, who had spent most of his life soldiering, should want military men about him, both for their compatibility and his security. Colonel Richard Levenson, who lived at 16 Kensington Square for about a year from 1697, had foiled an assassination plot against the King the previous year. Lady Mary Kirke, the first resident at no. 9, from 1693-7, was the widow of Colonel Percy Kirke of 'Kirke's lambs', who slaughtered the rebels after Sedgemoor and later influenced the Army in William's cause.

Royal retainers in the Square included, at no. 25, the King's barber who lived rent free and received an allowance for combs, looking glasses and wash bowls. James and Elizabeth Worthington, surmised to be a husband and wife, Groom of the Back Stairs and Laundress to the Queen's Court, and Peter Guenon de Beaubuisson, Gentleman of the Guns, Master of the King's Setting Dogs and Keeper of the Private Armoury, are recorded at several addresses in the first years of the eighteenth century.

Two houses were reserved specifically to house some of the Maids of Honour when the Court was at Kensington. It is thought that this may have given rise to the story that the ageing courtesan, the Duchess of Mazarin, may have lived there for a while, whereas it is more likely that it was one of her servants.

A later courtesan, one of George II's many amours, Camilla, Dowager Countess of Tankerville, lived at no. 13 from 1772 to 1775. Walpole assured the Queen that Lady Tankerville was 'a very safe fool who would give the King some amusement without giving her Majesty any trouble'.

After the death of Queen Caroline, in 1737, George II took a dislike to Kensington where he had lived happily, if not faithfully, with his wise, kindly 'fat Venus'. His presence thereafter, and of course that of his Court, in Kensington was infrequent. "Scarcely enough company to pay for lighting the candles", said Walpole.

THE GREAT AND THE GOOD

Although some of the Square's larger houses were converted into schools, it continued to attract the great and the good from different walks of life.

No. 18 was from 1837 to 1851 the home of John Stuart Mill, the philosopher and journalist, friend and colleague of Jeremy Bentham, the founder of 'Utilitarianism' – the promotion of the greatest happiness of the greatest number. Mill's famous 'System of Logic' was written while he lived there but the house is better known for the literary

18. Dr John Merriman jnr., also a local historian and local photographer.

calamity that happened there in 1835. Carlyle's manuscript of the first volume of his *History of the French Revolution* was inadvertently burnt by a maid who mistook the scattered papers for kindling. Mill had to take a cab to Carlyle's home in Chelsea and tell him what had happened and offer him £100 as compensation.

Richard Blackmore, Physician to William III, is known to have lived in the Square, though no specific address is recorded, and was among the first of its several famous medical residents. Most important among these must be the Merriman family, who occupied no. 45 for ninety years from 1805. They were John Merriman (1779-1839) his sons John Merriman junior, and James Nathaniel Merriman all of whom held the position of medical attendant to the Royal Family and Apothecary General to Queen Victoria. Their house backed on to that of Thackeray in Young Street. John Merriman junior was also a keen historian and pioneer photographer. His records of the neighbourhood in Victorian times have provided a unique archive much of which he bequeathed to Kensington Libraries.

Another famous Victorian doctor, Sir John Simon, a pioneer in sanitary reform and pathologist, lived at no. 40 from 1863 to 1903. Dr James Veitch, the naval surgeon who revolutionised surgery by his

use of ligatures and who introduced inoculation to the Navy, lived at no. 33 from 1841-47. When house hunting in 1860 Sir Edward Burne-Jones, visited Kensington Square 'lying back undisturbed from the world with nothing but gardens between it and the narrow High Street.' He took no. 41 for a while and William Morris, whom they called 'Topsy', gave him and his wife a Persian carpet.

The famous actress, Mrs Patrick Campbell, lived at no. 33 from 1898 to 1918, drifting about the neighbourhood in trails of lace with her adored dog, Pinky Poo. Hers was the house which the financier and philanthropist, Angus Ackworth, who lived there from 1927 to 1958, gave to the National Trust. A prominent member of the Georgian Group, he was in the forefront of those who fought to save the Square from its commercial spoilers, particularly the Barker group, a battle that went on for nearly a century.

FIGHTING BARKERS

As early as 1890 the expanding empire of John Barker was encroaching on the Square, with horses and delivery vans stabled in the south-east corner, in the mews that Young had intended for the carriages of his wealthy residents. By 1914 the firm owned houses all round the Square which they used either as hostels or offices. The invasion was particularly aggressive on the north side where they attempted to buy Thackeray's old house and also those once occupied by the Merriman family so as to build a loading bay. Stirred into action, many owners in the Square agreed to sign covenants restricting occupation of the properties to private use. Nevertheless by 1939 Barker's claimed to own two thirds of the north side.

After a war-time truce, the battle recommenced in 1946 when one of the first big planning battles of the post war years was fought. The LCC had already zoned the Square as a 'special business area' and in 1946 Kensington's Planning Committee said that there was no substantial reason for the preservation of the buildings on either architectural or historical grounds. One member of the Council declared that its beauty was over-rated. The interiors included, she said, dust-collecting panelling and filigree work, and cold veined marble mantelpieces and the flat-faced exteriors were grim and grey. Happily this opinion was not shared by her fellow members who rejected the committee's report by a large majority. In 1968, Kensington Square was declared the second of the Borough's new Conservation Areas.

When Thomas Young made his first plans for his 'noble square' in 1686 they included a central garden 'simply laid to lawn, edged with a single

19. A John Barker delivery van at the south-west corner of Kensington Square, in 1910.

row of trees.' Early in its history rules were laid down to ensure that it was preserved, with no swine allowed to wander, horses exercised or carpets beaten. Those employed to tend it did so faithfully. Arthur Ponsonby recalled Brinkworth, who had worked there for thirty-five years and his predecessor, Taverner, for forty.

Thomas Young was not so lucky with the Spring Garden and Bowling Green. These were let to market gardeners until the railway divided them in two, half becoming part of the grounds of the Assumption Convent and the rest coal yards, until the modern hotel was built.

THE GREYHOUND

Although disparagingly described by Angela Thirkell as a 'commonplace gin palace', The Greyhound is one of the luckier remnants of the area. The original house of this name goes back to the early days of Kensington Square. In 1710 Benjamin Jackman took out an insurance policy from the Greyhound Tavern but it is known to have existed

some ten years earlier. The manor courts were sometimes held there in the eighteenth century. Alterations were made to the original building but the big change came with its Victorian rebuilding which Miss Thirkell, who lived next door, deplored. In 1977 it was badly damaged by a gas explosion but has been restored.

SOUTH END

The 'Paradise garden' was no more, but the walk to it, South End, remained as a cul-de-sac. Here, a small piece of land became the site of a house occupied by Sir George Baker, a royal physician and a pioneer researcher into lead poisoning, from 1772-1779. South End itself was occupied until the end of the nineteenth century by nothing more than stables and outbuildings of the houses in Kensington Square, plus a rag and bone merchant and a coffee-house for workmen. It was not until main drainage was installed with a visible sewer vent pipe, that more building was possible, such as St Albans Studios.

20. The Greyhound, c.1870.

Up to the end of the Second World War this quiet cul-de-sac retained an old world charm with a sweet shop and cobbler's round the corner, even if the stables had become garages. It was still village-like, saved by its inaccessibility, but in the early 1990s plans, opposed by conservationists, resulted in its redevelopment.

THE STREET OF SHOPS

The name of Young Street dates from the very earliest days of Thomas Young's enterprise, most of its first buildings being erected while he was imprisoned in the Fleet.

Very few of the original houses remain. These include no. 16 (then 13) the home of William Makepeace Thackeray, for seven years from 1846 to 1853. Apart from this and one or two other houses it was mainly a street of tradespeople which by the 1870s included a cheesemonger, smithy, butcher, slaughter house and three apothecaries. In 1885 a block of flats, Kensington Square Mansions, was built next to no. 16 and a new post office

replaced the Victorian building until that too went for the modern multi-storey car park.

In its early days Young Street was the only road to Kensington Square from the High Street, but in 1728, a little by-way, today's Derry Street, was opened up on the west side of the Square.

Barker's demolished two early houses, nos. 25 and 27 Young Street. The latter was the home of Thackeray's daughter, Anne Ritchie, from 1878 to 1884 and later of the classical scholar, J. W. Mackail, whose daughter, Angela Thirkell, wrote of her childhood there in *Three Houses* (1931). Barker's wish to extend their bakery behind it and its neighbouring houses on the east side of Young Street was unopposed by the LCC although a fight to save them was waged by conservationists.

A later resident of Thackeray's own house was the painter, G.B. O'Neill, father of the composer, Norman O'Neill. Barker's bought the freehold of the house in 1924 and used it for various office departments during which fears for its future never abated despite the blue plaque on its then sooty frontage.

21. *Back street shops in South End.   Drawing by Frank L. Emanuel, 1930.*

22. *South End, 1909.*

THACKERAY'S HOME

Thackeray's seven years at no. 16 Young Street were probably the happiest in his life for it was there that he was re-united with his two little daughters, Anne (Pussy) and Harriet (Minnie) aged eleven and six. They had been living with his parents in Paris since his young wife, Isabella, had been struck with mental illness – probably schizophrenia – since the younger child's birth.

After early days of poverty he was making a name as a journalist on *Punch* and other magazines and by 1846 he was affluent enough to take a house in London where he could lead a family life. 'I am child sick' he told a friend. The bow-fronted house in Young Street was all that he wanted. 'When I caught sight of its two bulging half towers which flank the central doorway I thought it had the air of a feudal castle and exclaimed 'I'll have a flag staff over the coping and hoist a standard.'

His daughter, who herself became a well known author, wrote in her memoirs of her father: 'Once more he had a home and a family, two young children, three servants and a little black cat'. He hung pictures on the schoolroom walls that he thought would please them. There were two doves in a wicker cage and a garden 'which although not tidy was full of sweet things, verbenas, red and blue and scented, stacks of flags and bunches of London Pride'.

Here, in a study facing west across the garden, Thackeray wrote the highly successful *Vanity Fair*, *Pendennis* and *Henry Esmond*. In between there were trips with the children, by omnibus or 'fly' – he later had his own carriage – and visits from most of the famous personalities of the day. These included a rather disappointing evening when the guests included Charlotte Brontë. 'A tiny delicate little person, pale, with straight fair hair and steady eyes'. The conversation was so dull that Thackeray crept quietly out to his club.

Apart from his novels, Thackeray was now editor of the new and successful *Cornhill Magazine* and in 1853 he left Young Street for Onslow Square which he thought might be a more fashionable address for his growing-up daughters. They all returned to the centre of Kensington in 1860 when he was attracted to the tumble-down house on Palace Green, which in the end he had to rebuild. His health was now failing – he had contracted chronic malaria – and he died four years later, on Christmas Eve 1863 at the age of 52.

23. Thackeray's house at 16 Young Street.

The Queenly Palace

'Kingly Kensington' Dean Swift called it, but Kensington owes most of its fame to queens and princesses.

The royal association began with William III and Queen Mary, who were both grandchildren of Charles I. William suffered from chronic asthma and the 'smoak of London much incommoded him', so the couple sought a winter house not too far from the seat of government at Westminster as an alternative to Whitehall. Nottingham House, set in parkland between the two western roads, was the 'only retreat that pleased them.' A modest country house, it was obtained in 1689 for £18,000 from the 2nd Earl of Nottingham. Christopher Wren, although still occupied with St Paul's, was commissioned to improve it with all haste as Queen Mary was impatient to move in, staying temporarily at nearby Holland House from whence she could 'go often to hasten the workmen.'

Details survive of the work carried out, including the building of Clock Court, the Queen's Gallery and the chapel (probably that of the old house, refurbished, and later destroyed by Queen Victoria's mother who needed more space.) Also installed were two cisterns and washers and a 'stoole' for the Queen with a velvet covered seat!

Not all went smoothly. Very early on a newly erected building collapsed, with deaths and injuries among the workmen, and the following year a fire broke out on the south side of Clock Court 'diligently dealt with by footguards.'

William was still the soldier he had been all his life and his active part in campaigns in Europe and Ireland often took him away from England for long periods. During these times Mary came out of the shadows of wifely subordination and dealt competently with affairs of state but still found time to ward off loneliness by her interest in the gardens surrounding her new home. She called in the famous Brompton gardener, Henry Wise, to redesign the views from the Palace windows to resemble the formal Dutch beds at the King's old home in Holland.

Neither William nor Mary were robust. Apart from asthma, William probably also suffered from chronic anaemia and Mary was still childless after numerous miscarriages. William took a mistress and Mary concentrated on her furnishings, silks and brocades, her huge collection of china, and the gardens. When she was taken ill with smallpox William had a camp bed moved into her room during her last days, becoming increasingly distraught. She died, aged 32, in December 1694 and

24. *William III; portrait by an unknown artist.*

for months after he was in a state of nervous collapse, leaving Kensington to live at Richmond. When he did return to Kensington, he channelled his grief into renewed efforts to improve the palace, most notably directing that Wren's original plan for the Grand Staircase and King's Gallery should go ahead as well as the range of the buildings on the south side. William Kent would later enhance these additions with lavish decorations.

During the year that William and Mary had moved into Kensington Palace, Mary's sister, Anne, had given birth to a son, William Henry, Duke of Gloucester, her fifth child and the only survivor of many still births and miscarriages. In 1690 she and her husband, Prince George of Denmark, took up residence at Campden House, less than half a mile from the Palace, on the hill above Kensington village. From the beginning the baby was sickly, suffering from fevers and fits: today we know he was hydrocephalus (suffering from water on the brain). Although delicate, he had a strong will and high spirits and was spoilt and pampered by his anxious parents who indulged his every whim. Among the more extravagant of these fancies was the assembly of a large group of little boys with whom he could realise his military obsession by

The Royal Palace of KINGSIN

25. *'The Royal Palace of Kingsington', a print sold at the end of the seventeenth century.*

drills and parades, one of which took place before his Uncle William at Kensington Palace.

The King, who favoured the little boy, was enchanted, but not with his mother who was already under the influence of the powerful Sarah Jennings, later Duchess of Marlborough. The boy's health was of great importance since, after the death of Mary, he was in direct line to the throne, but in 1700, the day after his eleventh birthday, the boy fell ill and died a few days later.

Within two years William too was dead, having broken his collar bone and contracted pneumonia. Poor, plain, fat Queen Anne, who inherited the throne, worn down by her constant pregnancies and frequently ill, left Kensington two great legacies, the splendid Orangery designed by Christopher Wren and modified by Vanbrugh, and her extensive work on the gardens.

GERMAN GEORGE

Anne's last act was to secure the Protestant succession via the House of Hanover, although this meant a King who could not speak English and who had to conduct affairs of state in bad Latin. So German George came to Kensington, finding it very much to his liking since it was similar to his country estate in Hanover.

History has very little good to say about him. He was it seems, dull, unpleasant, greedy, sensual, immoral, and drank heavily. He shut up his ill-used wife in a German castle but he did lavish much care and expense on Kensington Palace.

The core of the old building was replaced by two new courts, one specifically intended for occupation by his mistress, the Duchess of Kendal, who had come over from Germany with him, together with the rest of an enormous retinue of retainers. These included some very strange supernumaries, such as Jory the Dwarf, who behaved so badly he had to be shut up in the East wing, and a Wild Boy who had been found in the woods near Hamelin and roamed Kensington Gardens like an 18th-century Tarzan, swinging from the trees.

While the King was busy with plans for the Cupola Room, Drawing Room and Privy Chamber and arranging ornate decorations by William Kent he was also quarrelling with his son, the Prince of Wales. He expelled him and his wife, the Princess Caroline, from Kensington and took their children into his own custody.

The King collapsed and died on his way to Germany in 1727 and the younger George and his Queen moved into the Palace from which they had been banished, their arrival ushering in its greatest age. Their life there has been faithfully chronicled. It lacked nothing in gossip, intrigue, scandal and family rows. Most of it centred around another

26. *Kensington Palace from the south in the eighteenth century.*

Prince of Wales, Frederick William, who was also expelled from Court but died before he could become King.

George and Caroline had been married for over twenty years before they came to the throne. She was an intelligent and attractive woman, though on the large side, but she had good taste and patronised the leading architects and artists of the day. She did much to build up the Royal Collection of pictures not least by her find in a drawer of a collection of some hundred or so Holbein drawings now at Windsor. Her other passion was gardening and she originated many of the present delights of Kensington Gardens.

Although George adored his wife he was constantly unfaithful, testing her forbearance to the limit by consulting her on his mistresses. She in turn got great support from her faithful friend and advisor Robert Walpole. In 1737 she fell ill with what was at first diagnosed as colic but turned out to be a strangulated hernia. Dosed with preparations such as Snake Root, and bled, she died on 20 November. The King continued to live at Kensington for much of the year during the rest of his long life. He died there suddenly on 25 October 1760. There are stories of his ghost appearing at the oval window in the Clock Tower.

REGENCY SCANDALS

It was the King's grandson who became George III. Many years earlier he had told Walpole he wished to be excused living at Kensington. The State Rooms were closed and for the next sixty years the Palace stood virtually empty. It was not until 1808, when the relationship between the Prince of Wales (the Regent) and his wife, the eccentric Caroline of Brunswick, was becoming intolerable, that the wild lady was offered apartments there.

Caroline's behaviour and morals shocked society but she enjoyed enormous public support. She lived at Kensington until 1814. Included in her household was a boy, William Austin, who was suspected as being her illegitimate son and the subject of what was called the 'Delicate Investigation'. After a spell abroad, she returned to England shortly before George IV's coronation. The country was divided between her and her unpopular husband who took out a Bill of Divorcement in the House of Lords. Refused admission to his coronation, she died a few weeks later and her ghost is said to haunt Princess Margaret's apartments at Kensington.

The Duke of Sussex, George III's sixth son and the Regent's brother, was Caroline's neighbour while she lived at Kensington Palace, occupying

27. *The Cupola room at Kensington Palace, c.1898*

28. *The Duke of Sussex in his library.*

apartments in the southern range of Clock Court. A rebel himself, he was one of her staunchest supporters. Another asthmatic, with poor sight, he built up a library of fifty thousand books in the Long Gallery as well as a collection of clocks and watches. He contracted three illegal marriages, two to the same woman.

Princess Sophia, George III's delicate and near blind daughter, took up residence in the northeast corner of Clock Court before moving to York House in 1839.

In 1819, Edward, Duke of Kent, another of the Regent's formerly promiscuous brothers, was now a respectable married man by order. Well aware of the dynastic implications, he brought his heavily pregnant wife from Germany to his apartments at Kensington Palace. On 24 May 1819, a daughter was born in a dressing room there. The christening in the Cupola Room was the scene of a family argument over names, the eventual choice being Alexandrina Victoria, although it was by the latter she was known.

The Duke of Kent, impecunious as ever, died nine months later and the little Princess was brought up by her mother at Kensington. She was not an exemplary child: she shouted at servants and had appalling table manners, but she was diligent at her studies.

There was no love lost between the Princess's mother and William IV, who on a visit to the Palace was incensed to find that the Duchess had

29. The Duchess of Kent with Princess Victoria. Drawing by George Hayter, c.1834.

30. Princess Louise in 1871.

appropriated an extra seventeen rooms.

It was at Kensington, a year before she became Queen, that Victoria had her first meeting with Prince Albert – 'so handsome, so full of goodness and sweetness and very clever and intelligent.'

On 20 June 1837, King William died and in the small hours of the morning the historic interview took place when Victoria was told she was Queen. In her diary on 13 July 1837, she recorded her departure from Kensington. 'It was the last time that I slept in this poor old Palace as I am to go to Buckingham Palace today ... it is not without feelings of regret that I bid adieu for ever ... to this my birthplace ... to which I am really attached...'

A ROYAL FAMILY HOME

Although she rarely visited the Palace she maintained an interest in it, ensuring it was kept in as good a state of repair as funds allowed. A variety of schemes for its use were put forward, including use as the National Gallery or a home for Florence Nightingale.

But the Queen would not countenance these, and the necessity to find homes for an extensive royal family solved the question of its use. Among the first to arrive, in 1867, were the Prince and

Princess of Teck – the Princess, Mary Adelaide, being the cousin of the Queen. They were expecting their first child, who turned out to be a girl and strengthened the Palace's connection with queens, for she was to become Queen Mary, wife of George V. Known as Princess May, the little girl spent her babyhood in Kensington.

Despite their debts, the Tecks' life style was extravagant. This led to the famous anecdote which relates how the Duchess, speaking at the opening of a new church hall in Kensington to which John Barker had generously contributed, proposed a vote of thanks 'to Mr Barker to whom we all owe so much.' Fortunately perhaps for Mr Barker, the Tecks were not long at Kensington, leaving when May was only fourteen months old.

In 1873, soon after her marriage to the Marquess of Lorne, Princess Louise, Victoria's artistic sixth child, moved in. The marriage had been hastily arranged because of rumours circulating about Louise's unsuitable attachments to men, in particular the sculptor Sir Edgar Boehm, her tutor at South Kensington Art School. The marriage was not a success and they became estranged in 1880 although they both continued to live at Kensington Palace. She was a talented sculptress as can be seen by the fine statue of her mother, which stands today facing the Round Pond in Kensington

Gardens. Boehm's sudden death in his Fulham Road studio caused a scandal as the Princess was present at the time. Not surprisingly this generated press interest, some of it suggestive, although Louise insisted that he had collapsed while carrying a heavy bust which brought about a heart aneurysm; this was also the coroner's verdict.

There was also the matter of the bricked-up window in the apartments now occupied by Princess Margaret. It is beyond doubt that this was done on Louise's orders to keep her husband from wandering in the grounds. Whether this was to prevent him from chasing men or women or to counter the early stages of Alzheimer's Disease is not clear but it once again provided the subject of gossip. History, and certainly the residents of Kensington, prefer to remember the Princess as a skilled painter and her many good works and charities, including the Princess Louise Hospital for Children in North Kensington. She continued to live at the Palace until her death in 1939.

By the 1890s the condition of the Palace was causing concern. Repairs to the State Rooms and the Orangery were undertaken and paintings, mainly of historical interest, were brought back from Windsor. On the Queen's eightieth birthday the State Rooms were open to the public, this being the condition of the £23,000 grant by Parliament towards the cost of the restoration. *The Times* disclosed that there had been a plan to demolish the old building and said 'the public owed a debt of gratitude to the Queen for having strenuously resisted such an act of vandalism.' Victoria made a last visit to the Palace only a few days before her birthday. Fortunately she had not seen it before the work was begun or it might have broken her heart. The report on its condition stated that the Queen's Staircase had presented 'a woeful state of dust, filth, decay and rot, the fine iron balustrades were broken and damp was oozing from the walls, with tattered strips of canvas.

Princess Beatrice, the youngest of Queen Victoria's large family, had become the Queen's closest companion ever since the death of Albert and even more so since the death of John Brown in 1883. When she married Prince Henry of Battenberg, the Queen begged the young couple to live with her at Windsor, Balmoral and Osborne. The Prince died of malaria in 1896 and Beatrice came to live at Kensington Palace. She died in 1944.

Her great nephew, Prince Philip, stayed at the Palace with the Dowager Marchioness of Milford Haven, his grandmother, and mother of Earl Mountbatten, on many occasions during his boyhood and it was here that he spent the night before his wedding to the Princess Elizabeth in 1947.

Work on the restoration of the Palace continued

31. Clock Court c.1905.

during the reign of Edward VII and more of it was opened to the public. In 1911, just after the King's death, the London Museum was established there, mainly in the State Apartments. Although moved to Stafford (Lancaster) House in 1913, it returned to Kensington in 1956 before its permanent installation as the Museum of London in the Barbican in 1975.

'THE AUNT HEAP'

In 1917 this royal enclave was increased when the Duchess of Albany, widow of Victoria's youngest son, Leopold and their daughter, Princess Alice, moved into Clock House. Princess Alice made Kensington her permanent home for the rest of her long life. She died aged 97 in 1981 and it was she in her memoirs who disclosed the Palace's nickname of the 'Aunt Heap.'

During the First World War thousands of parcels were sent out from the Palace to Irish soldiers and prisoners of war from a depot at which both Queen Mary and her daughters, Princess Mary, later Princess Royal, worked as volunteers.

In 1955, Princess Marina, the Duchess of Kent, moved into the Palace with her children until they married and in the 1970s Prince and Princess Michael of Kent also came to live there. Princess Margaret had been in residence since the 1960s with her children and the Palace also became the home of the Duke and Duchess of Gloucester. Princess Alice, Duchess of Gloucester, remained after the Duke's death and their son the present Duke of Gloucester is still there with his wife.

Most famously of course, in the 1980s the Palace became the home of the Prince and Princess of Wales and their two sons Prince William and Prince Harry. After the end of their marriage, Diana, Princess of Wales continued to live at Kensington Palace. The tragic events that followed have written a new chapter in the 300 years of the building's history.

Around Parson's Yard

John Jones and his nephew and son-in-law, John Price, were bricklayers who in 1724 had accumulated enough to buy land from their more aristocratic neighbours. Jones had already acquired the freehold of the Crown Inn, formerly The Angel, on the corner of Church Street and the High Street where he had built fourteen houses known as Jones' Buildings in the stable yard. The arched entrance to these still remains, although rebuilt in 1872. His later acquisitions extended further north and west to take in the Parsonage House and Parson's Yard, which was to be known as Holland Street from 1821. The parsonage is believed to have been situated between Gregory Place and Church Walk and by then was in secular occupation as the Vicars had moved to another house a century or so earlier.

Here Jones began to build, firstly along Church Street's western side. Of these houses only six remain, nos. 9-17, hardly recognisable today with shops on their ground floors. On the corner of Holland Street is the old George Inn, later renamed the Catherine Wheel, rebuilt in 1870. In Holland Street itself Jones built on both sides, although none of the six cottages survives. There is thought to be a vestige of the stable yard, which was behind those on the north, in the weatherboard building in Holland Place known until a few years ago as the Dolls House.

In the midst of all this building Jones was involved in a dispute with his neighbour at Campden House, Lord Lechmore. It had begun when Jones pulled down a wall so that he could build on what is now Duke's Lane, which Lechmore considered a private way to his property. Jones also brought carts carrying building materials along this lane which his neighbour considered to be 'a forcible and riotous entry' and two Justices of the Peace and a constable were called in the next day when Lechmore's men stopped two such carts at the lane entrance.

The story continues that Jones' men 'made very loud Huzzas and Shouts', together with insulting remarks about the Justices, Lord Lechmore and his men, namely an 'unseemly fracas with much rudeness and sauciness.' Jones was having his hair cut at a neighbouring barbershop, but hearing the commotion outside came out and climbing on the scaffolding encouraged his labourers to continue their harangue, whereupon he was fined £20

32. *Nos. 1-5 Kensington Church Street., which were built c.1760.*

on the spot. Refusing to pay, a constable was ordered to take him in a cab to Newgate Prison.

This ignominy was avoided, but the case did go to Chancery. The outcome is unknown but the whole affair may have had a bad affect on Jones' health, as he died a few months later in March 1727. Jones bequeathed the estate to his wife and John Price. Building continued for the next ten years or so, after which there was a lull when some parts were sold off to other developers. Happily, a great many of these early 18th-century houses remain, despite some alterations and repairs. The Parsonage House was left in trust for Jones' grandchildren and there is no firm date for its demolition, although by 1760 Price had built six new houses with gardens which covered the site, having earlier disposed of the rest to the parish to extend the churchyard.

BEAUTIFUL SOCIALIST

These houses were nos. 1-7 (odd) Church Street and two in Holland Street. Of the latter no. 13 remains which from 1894 to 1915 was the home of the artist Walter Crane. Although best known as a children's book illustrator, Crane was also a designer of exquisite ceramics, a creator of mosaics and a producer of art work for the Socialist

33. *An invitation to a tennis party at Church Walk Garden, the site of today's Ingelow House, c1882. In the left foreground is a mock gravestone dedicated to 'the Misguided Man who wildly shied all the tennis balls over the wall.'*

Movement he espoused.

Born in 1845, he reached maturity at a time when the technicalities of printing and engraving underwent great changes and as one of the younger members of the Arts and Crafts Movement he drew on his romantic imagination rather than medieval images.

His early books, such as *Mother Hubbard*, depict beautifully dressed people living in ideal places, and his work was very popular with his contemporaries who used it to decorate their homes. He also designed leaflets and banners for trade unions. 'Solidarity of Labour' was one of twelve drawings he made to commemorate the International Socialist Workers and Trades Union Congress in 1896, the year of William Morris's death.

In 1897 he was appointed Principal of the Royal College of Art, a position he held for a fairly short time but during which he was able to promote his theories on the reform of teaching and the development of industrial design.

AROUND CHURCH WALK

Church Walk was an old cartway leading from the Parsonage to the High Street. The present alley, which runs beside the old Vestry Hall (now the Melli Bank), was not made until the parish bought a piece of land called Paramour's Pingle as a burial ground extension. The name is derived from its previous tenant, Lawrence Paramour.

A resident in the 1830s and 40s was the poet, Jean Ingelow; she is commemorated in the name of the flats now standing on the site of her home.

The building of the Metropolitan Railway caused considerable disruption in the neighbourhood as

34. Holland Street in the 1940s.

the cut-and–cover tunnellers dug their way beneath the High Street, bringing about the end of the old Hornton Street Chapel and school, and some houses in Lower Phillimore Place.

Opposite where Holland Street meets Church Street, the land was occupied by the 'forcing grounds', or kitchen gardens, of Kensington Palace. Originally known as the More, this four-acre field was renamed Conduit Close after the brick structure in its north-east corner, said to have been built for Henry VIII's water supply to his palace in Chelsea. In the 1660s Thomas Hodges built two houses on it, the successors of which, about a century later, were to become York House and Maitland House.

George III's daughter, Princess Sophia, occupied York House from 1839 until her death in 1848. Maitland House was the home of John Stuart Mill and his father, John Mill, and later the artist David Wilkie. The houses were replaced in 1904 by York House flats and the block of showrooms and offices first built for the Gas Light & Coke Co. in 1924.

THE BARRACKS
In the late 1840s the Crown Commissioners leased the old forcing grounds to the War Office to replace the Guards Barracks facing Palace Green. The new buildings were to be 'in a plain but good style'. There were two blocks, one for cavalry and another for infantry. For many years the Barracks were occupied by the Royal Army Service Corps and in its last years by the Royal Military Police.

35. Maitland House, Church Street, the home of John Stuart Mill and the artist, David Wilkie.

In the 1960s the Soviets, having outgrown their premises in Kensington Palace Gardens, showed great interest in the Barracks site for a new embassy but the plan was dropped and a controversial scheme for shops, flats and offices was given approval instead.

VICARAGES

The east side of Church Street was land assigned to the vicar of Kensington as part of his benefice. At least four vicarages were built on its southern portion. The early 17th-century house stood at the junction with Vicarage Gate. Its successor was Georgian and in 1887 a new house was erected further to the east where the present Vicarage and Parish Hall now stand in the Vicarage Gate cul-de-sac.

36. *Houses on the south side of Holland Street, drawn c.1937.*

37. *Lord Strathcona addressing Canadian soldiers at Kensington Barracks after the presentation of medals at Buckingham Palace.*

38. *Kensington Canal, looking south to Brompton Cemetery; by William Cowen c.1841.*

Up the Creek

THE KENSINGTON CANAL

Various names have defined the stream which is Kensington's western boundary – but it is now demoted to a sewer. Known in several sections as Billingswell Ditch, Bull or Counters Creek, it flowed from springs at Kensal Green. Then it passed through the woods north of Shepherds Bush and the marshes of Notting Dale, through the pastures of the Holland Estate to Chelsea and its outlet to the Thames just before Lacey's Point.

At Kensington, the main highway west from London towards Hammersmith and Acton crossed the creek at Countesses Bregge, recorded in 1421 when the Countess of Oxford, the then owner of Earls Court Manor, was called upon to repair it. Today it is known as Addison Bridge.

At the beginning of the eighteenth century, the creek was still a sylvan stream where Joseph Addison, then dwelling for a while at a house beside it, could write of larks and nightingales singing there. Its industrialisation began when William Edwardes, the 2nd Earl Kensington, owner of the estate which stretched from Fulham Road to Kensington's main thoroughfare, decided that if the creek, reasonably navigable as far as Stamford Bridge, could be canalised, it would provide a reliable outlet for goods to the Thames and greatly enhance the value of his property.

The Kensington Canal Company applied for parliamentary permission to do this work in 1824. The Company consisted of Lord Kensington and Sir John Scott Lillie, owner of the land on the other side of the stream in Fulham, and sixteen other investors. Two of these were members of the prosperous Brindley shipbuilding family who were already engaged in building developments near the bridge at Kensington.

From the start the venture was beset by disaster. It was grossly under-financed, so eventually the builders went bankrupt; nevertheless the canal was completed and opened on 12 August 1828. *The Times* reported the celebration which took place 'on a stately barge proceeding from Battersea'

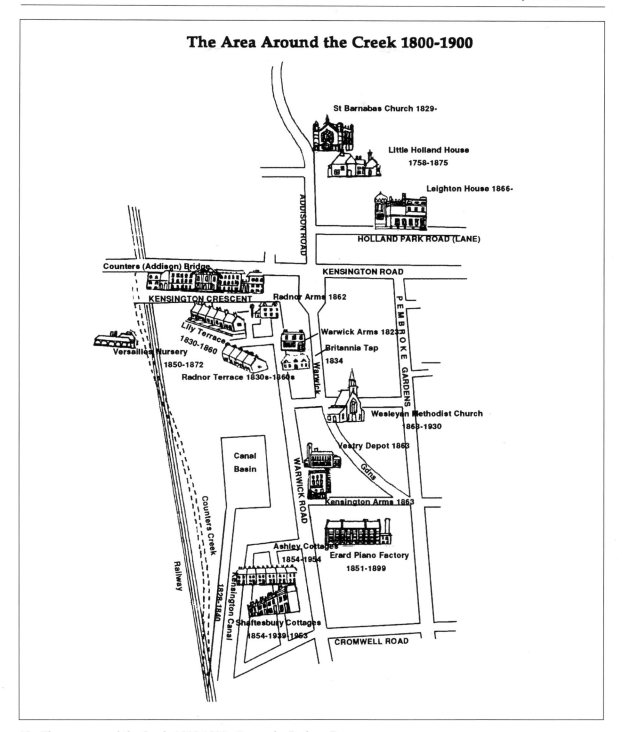

The Area Around the Creek 1800-1900

St Barnabas Church 1829-

Little Holland House
1758-1875

Leighton House 1866-

ADDISON ROAD

HOLLAND PARK ROAD (LANE)

Counters (Addison) Bridge

KENSINGTON ROAD

KENSINGTON CRESCENT

Radnor Arms 1862

PEMBROKE GARDENS

Lily Terrace
1830-1860

Warwick Arms 1823

Versailles Nursery
1850-1872

Britannia Tap
1834

Radnor Terrace 1830s-1860s

Warwick

Wesleyan Methodist Church
1863-1930

Vestry Depot 1863

Gdns

Canal
Basin

WARWICK ROAD

Kensington Arms 1863

Counters Creek

Ashley Cottages
1854-1954

Erard Piano Factory
1851-1899

Railway

Kensington Canal
1828-1840

Shaftesbury Cottages
1854-1939 1953

CROMWELL ROAD

39. *The area around the Creek, 1800-1900. Drawn by Barbara Denny.*

which sailed up the canal 'amidst cheers of the multitude assembled' this being followed in the evening by a sumptuous dinner. The 200 or so work people had their own party assisted by the gift of a butt of porter.

The canal, 1³/₄ miles long and 100 feet wide, allowed the passage of barges up to 100 tons burthen and culminated in a basin about 300 yards south of the Kensington bridge, approximately the position of today's Pembroke Road. But its life was pathetically short. By the mid 1830s it had been described as a 'total failure' by Lord Holland, who owned the land to the north of the bridge through which any extension of the canal towards the Grand Junction Canal at Paddington would have to pass. In 1840 there were further problems when its existing length was badly affected by tidal variations, cutting its viable hours of operation.

No wonder the promoters of the venture were relieved to be approached by a group of railway entrepreneurs, including Lord Kensington's son and heir, the Hon. Captain William Edwardes, Sir John Lillie and the Earls Court land owner, Robert Gunter, wishing to purchase the canal land for the construction of their proposed Birmingham, Bristol & Thames Junction line.

Lord Holland, fearing for the amenities of his estate, predicted that the railway would prove as signal a failure as the canal. He was not far wrong, for although the railway opened in May 1844 its subsequent history was unstable and constantly subject to changes in use and ownership (*see* pp76-77). But it set the seal on the final industrial and residential development of what had been until then an area of market gardens, orchards and small-holdings.

BUILDING AROUND WARWICK GARDENS

Development had already begun some years earlier when the Brindleys had invested heavily in land between the canal and Edwardes Square. The ground leased to them by Lord Kensington consisted of eight acres with a frontage to the High Street from what is now St Mary Abbots Place to Warwick Road, extending south to the line of Pembroke Gardens.

The original intention was to construct a square for which Lord Kensington offered a site for a church on the southern side. This plan did not materialise but it accounts for the wide entrance to what was to become Warwick Gardens; it took nearly fifty years before the whole road was finally built up with its curving access to Pembroke Gardens. Lord Kensington also promised to disguise the open sewer on the eastern boundary by constructing a mound 'covered by forest trees'.

40. *Kensington Crescent c.1905, site of Charles House.*

This also never came about. This side of the site bounded on the 1¹/₂ acre garden of the Horticultural Society, which existed for about six years (1818 to 1824) before it moved to Chiswick. The site later became St Mary Abbots Place and 343-53 Kensington High Street with a market garden at the rear.

Within two years or so of its commencement, the Warwick Gardens development ran into severe financial difficulty exacerbated by the credit crisis of 1825, and in 1826 the Brindleys were declared bankrupt.

The intended central garden has a shadow today in the central flower bed and the 'chocolate stick' marble column. This was erected to the memory of Queen Victoria by the citizens of Kensington, and was moved there from its original site at the south end of Kensington Church Street in 1934. Lord Kensington died before the whole length of Warwick Gardens was completed but his son continued with the development.

The Methodists' decision to build chapels 'in more respectable situations' resulted in the construction of a handsome red brick, black-banded edifice on the corner of Pembroke Gardens and Warwick Gardens in 1862 (*see* p.128), but from the beginning it still drew its congregation from further afield, and in 1927 it closed, the site being sold for building more houses.

All the original houses on the east side of Warwick Gardens have survived apart from no.2, which was bombed during the Second World War. No. 11 was the home of G. K. Chesterton, poet, author and journalist (1874-1936) during his childhood and until his marriage in 1901 (*see* p48). On the west side, all the original houses as far as Pembroke Gardens have been replaced by blocks of flats. The first to go were nos. 2–26, demolished in 1926 to build St Mary Abbots Court. No. 2 had been the home in 1881 of William Holman Hunt, before he moved to Draycott Lodge in Fulham. More flats followed between 1930 and 1935 and Durrells House was built in 1971.

At the same time as the Brindleys were busy in Warwick Gardens, another developer was working on nine acres between there and the creek. He was Adam Tirrell, described variously as a gentleman and builder of Kensington, a farmer of Kent and a baker of Clerkenwell. He planned to build Kensington Crescent, 28 houses divided by a central road leading to a further development of about eighty smaller houses on narrow streets to the south. The Crescent was set back from the main road behind a narrow lawn and shrubbery. As the whole development was very soon to be within yards of the unsavoury stagnant canal basin it is not surprising that it was slow to sell and became even less attractive when the canal was drained and replaced by the railway and a coal depot.

Even ten years after the filling in of the canal basin, local residents were complaining about the 'putrid pool' of Warwick Road, probably caused by disused gravel pits which had been dug by the creek side. In the hot summer of 1855 there were letters to the *Kensington Gazette* about 'the suffocating stench of sewer discharge' and 'rotting animal carcasses', correspondents fearing for the

health of the hundred workers at the nearby piano factory.

Lord Kensington actually lived in one of the Crescent houses, no. 28, for about seven years, during which he became increasingly impoverished, until his death in 1852. Later residents of the Crescent included Sir William Siemens, the famous German-born electrical engineer and Kenneth Grahame, better known as the author of *The Wind in the Willows* than as secretary of the Bank of England, who lived at no. 5 from 1895 to 1900 before moving to Phillimore Place. The Crescent was demolished in the 1930s and the site remained vacant and semi-derelict for nearly twenty years until the building of Charles House, the government offices, in 1948-50.

The canal, and later the railway, had already spawned a hotchpotch of wharves warehouses and counting houses between the creek and the way between Warwick Gardens and Kensington Crescent, then known as Moiety Road. About a hundred working-class houses and cottages were to be built here, on what was to become Warwick Road, between the 1850s and 60s. Of these only a handful remain near the corner of West Cromwell Road.

This side of Warwick Road had been the site of Erards Piano Factory from 1851 to 1890 (*see* p.74),

41. Pembroke Road, c.1905.

42. *The Kensington Arms, c.1905.*

43. *Shaftesbury Cottages, Fenelon Place, 1954.*

44. *The Lock Keeper's Cottage.*

more small houses and a gravel pit. The Vestry, predecessor of the Council, already had a depot and stables on both sides of Pembroke Road in the 1860s and 70s. When the parish administration moved to the Town Hall this was greatly enlarged, firstly in 1912-14 and finally in the 1970s with the construction of the present huge building. This incorporates a transport depot, the refuse collection headquarters and high level housing, Chesterton Square and Broadwater Terrace. The exterior of this grim edifice viewed from Warwick Road frontage belies the pleasant seclusion of the internal garden enclosures high above the traffic.

In 1975 the Council also took over the former John Barker's furniture depository which had been established on part of the old piano factory site. The presence of so much thirsty industry may account for the proliferation of pubs in this area with no less than four within yards of each other, the Kensington Arms, on the corner of Pembroke Road, the Warwick Arms and the Britannia Tap, and opposite, the Radnor Arms. The latter is all that is left of Radnor Villas a small group of about fifteen houses here and in Lily Terrace and Wallis Cottages, demolished in the 1930s.

The slow progress of other more ambitious building projects had probably discouraged investment in further ventures of this kind and the remaining area between West Cromwell Road and Kensington High Street was abandoned to low price housing. However, one developer had more idealistic tendencies. He was Henry Benjamin Kent, a retired coal merchant, who with his step-son, a builder and house agent, erected some model cottages in 1851 to the south of the old canal basin which were a simpler version of the Prince Consort's model lodging houses displayed at the 1851 Exhibition. Called Shaftesbury Cottages after the philanthropist, Ashley Cooper, the 7th Earl, they stood on a narrow lane, which was later renamed Fenelon Place.

Very shortly after, in 1855, Kent entered into an agreement with Lord Kensington to develop the whole area and create a roadway on the line of the present West Cromwell Road extension. This development continued for over twenty years with a total of 120 houses, occupied, according to the

1871 census, by nearly 1000 people, an average of eight per house.

The residents were mainly labourers, with a high proportion of railway workers, building tradesmen and coal porters. Any remnants of these streets were swept away by the building of the Cromwell Road bridge in the 1940s although one pair survived to 1951 together with the recently demolished old lock-keeper's cottage, and part of the area was used for pre-fabricated housing.

In 1952 Warwick House, a block of Army married quarters, was built at the rear of Charles House but it had a short life, standing derelict for some years and amid criticism of housing wastage was eventually demolished. The 1960s saw large-scale developments, the new telephone exchange, a large garage and showrooms, and in the 1980s a Sainsbury's Homebase.

In the early 1990s what has become known as the Fenelon Place site has been the subject of a long running controversy. Two superstores, Safeway and Tesco, battled for its future use while the Council and the local residents worried over the escalation of traffic in this already heavily pressured area. The victors, Tesco, now have a huge building on the site.

LORD HOLLAND'S MEADOWS
The line of Kensington High Street and Addison Bridge marks the division of the Edwardes land from that of the Fox family, Lord Holland, having bought 200 acres of the original Holland House estate between Holland Walk and the creek in 1768. The creek here still flowed through pastures unsullied by development, grazed by the cows of Holland Farm and with names which tell their own pleasant story – Great and Little Rushy Fields, Washers Mead and the Fair Wild Hearts. Just east of Addison Bridge, the owners of James Lee's famous nursery rented a few acres for their splendid collection of plants. There was very little other building apart from Little Holland House (*see* pp105-106) and Mole House, believed by the historian, Thomas Faulkner, to be the remnant of the old Manor House of West Town. In the 1820s, at the same time as Edwardes was engaged on his entrepreneurial activities, the 3rd Lord Holland, grandson of Henry Fox, always short of money, was already building on other land he owned in Lambeth. Encouraged by the huge difference between agricultural and building rents (£4 compared to £18-20 an acre) he decided to speculate in Kensington, despite the opinion of his wife that 'none alive will be bettered by the undertaking.'

A law suit between the Fox and Edwardes families, which had dragged on for years, was finally settled and in 1824 building began on Addison Road, the first north/south thoroughfare to link the two old western highways, now known as Kensington High Street and Holland Park Avenue. Among the first buildings were five late Georgian houses, nos. 27–31, on the east side, demolished in the 1960s and replaced by a block of flats. Knocked down at the same time were four other cottage-type houses between the end of the terrace and Holland Park Road.

Progress was very slow, owing to the shortage of capital. Lady Holland complained that the cost of building a sewer was causing her sleepless nights. She wrote that 'the buildings are stopped in consequence of all the failures and panics, people have no money to spend on villas and keep closely what they have in the bank.' Lord Holland admitted to being short of money but he felt he 'was as well off as any of his friends and better off than most.' The advent of the railway company in 1836 provided a welcome bonus because the diversion and covering of the remains of Counters Creek necessitated the creation of a new sewer, for which the railway company had to bear the cost but Lord Holland had the most benefit.

However, an early plan to construct the line on a 23-foot high viaduct filled him with alarm. It would, he said, 'interrupt the view of the new houses and villas in Addison Road and the noise and smoke and other annoyances will drive the tenants from their habitations'.

His fears proved groundless as building continued in the late 1840s. St Barnabas Church, which opened in 1827 (*see* p.124) had already been described by *Building News* as 'ugly pseudo-gothic'. In 1857 the terrace of eight similar gothic houses, called then Warwick Villas, (nos. 40–47) received the same castigation. The journal considered them to be 'a debased Gothic style' adding that the cement used was also so poor that some of their gable ends had already fallen off.

The curve where St Barnabas Church now stands was necessitated by the circumnavigation of the ponds known as the moats, believed to be the original fish ponds where Sir Walter Cope had kept his cormorants two centuries earlier. They were later made into an ornamental lake by the owner of Oak Lodge, a large attractive house, the grounds of which covered the whole area of Oakwood Court, which replaced it in 1900.

Little Holland House, the old rambling building which in its last years was the home of the Prinseps family and G.F. Watts, was demolished in the 1870s for the construction of Melbury Road and the site is now largely occupied by the flats, Woodsford.

45. *The pseudo-Gothic houses of Warwick Villas in the 1940s. They are now renumbered as part of Addison Road.*

The site of the school for poor children which Caroline Fox had run while living at Little Holland House was sold to a riding school and later used to build six studios. Court House, built in 1929, is still approached through its arched entrance in Holland Park Road.

The development of the Holland Estate was almost entirely devoid of shops. Napier Road, a side turning at the southern end of Addison Road, has a short terrace backing on to the original Holland Mews (now Napier Place). A nursery garden on the north side became a builder's yard, which is now covered with a close of modern houses. The builders were Cockerells, originally of Barons Court, a business that included undertaking, the coffin carriers being used for ladders when that side of the business ended. Parsons, the butchers, had been there for decades and Farmers Library, the newsagents, had moved there from the High Street. The Crown & Sceptre pub at the corner of Holland Road was originally named the Napoleon III, a gesture towards the Holland family's admiration for the Bonapartes.

Between the mid 19th century and its close all the Holland farmland west of Addison Road to the now covered Creek/railway would be filled in with streets and houses. However to the east, a mixture of sentiment and circumstance preserved the magnificent parkland and the artists' enclave that was to enrich the southern acres around Leighton House (*see* p.108)

All Square

46. *Edwardes Square, c.1905.*

47. *A pageant by a children's theatre group in Edwardes Square, 1950s.*

EDWARDES SQUARE

Leigh Hunt is generally blamed for inventing, or at least encouraging and perpetuating, the myth that Edwardes Square, where he lived at 32 from 1840 to 1851, was built by a Frenchman anticipating the successful invasion by Napoleon's army and the occupying force requiring small houses near Kensington Palace, or more likely, Holland House, as the Hollands were Francophiles.

This story has long been scotched by the fact that Edwardes Square, the first of Lord Kensington's speculations, was not commenced until 1811 when the threat of invasion had disappeared. The builder was in truth an émigré Frenchman of somewhat dubious reputation, Louis Leon Changeur, who had fled the revolution but ended up in the Fleet Prison for reasons unchronicled. He has been

wrongly associated with another Frenchman of an even worse record, called Charmilly, denounced by Earl Grey as an 'infamous character'.

The original plan was to build about eighty houses around an exceptionally large garden on the eleven acres of land on the north-western corner of Lord Kensington's estate. The northern Earls Terrace side was to face the High Street but separated from it by a strip of trees and shrubbery with lodges each end, rows of 25 and 23 houses respectively on the east and west sides, and the south reserved for stables and coach houses. The financing of the ambitious scheme proved difficult and was aggravated by a building slump. In 1813 bankruptcy proceedings were taken against Changeur who owed a large amount of money to his principal co-developer, a lawyer, William Elderton Allen, among others. Both eventually fled to France but the financial misfortunes of the Square continued and the rate books show that by 1815 only 21 of the planned 81 houses were occupied and all those on the west side were empty.

In 1814 an advertisement offered the sale of four completed houses, nos. 14 to 17, and eight 'carcasses', the former 'fit for small respectable families'. In the midst of this debacle one participant remained stable, Daniel Sutton, a middle-aged carpet manufacturer from Wilton, near Salisbury. He was already involved in other building enterprises in London, and with his son of the same name became the chief developer of the whole Edwardes Square venture. He lived at three addresses there between 1813 and 1842, when he died at the age of 86, leaving property said to be worth half a million. It was to the Suttons and three other trustees that Lord Kensington leased the central garden and Earls Terrace shrubbery for ninety years from 1820 to 1910.

After 1815 things took a turn for the better and within six or seven years the Square had filled up and a further row of houses, Leonard's Terrace, built along the main road towards Earls Court Road, under the auspices of Sutton.

When Thomas Carlyle came to London from Scotland in search of a home in 1834 he viewed a house in the Square, no. 27, but was not impressed by it, although he had been attracted by the central garden. Describing the house in a letter he 'found the two kitchens much too low, only 6' 3"'; and the whole to have 'sorryish prospects', and rejected it in favour of Cheyne Row, Chelsea, where he lived for the rest of his life.

The garden which Carlyle liked so much had been laid out 'in a different manner from most other squares' by Anostino Aglio, the Italian artist and decorator, who lived at no. 15 from 1814 to 1820, with informal winding paths and an orna-

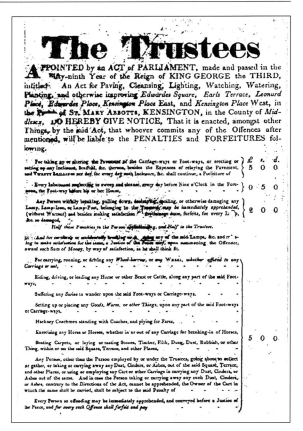

48. A notice issued by the Trustees in 1819 listing fines for offences in Edwardes Square. They prohibit Hackney cabs, wheelbarrows, pigs and beating carpets.

mental temple at the south end, used as a gardener's lodge.

In 1819 an Act of Parliament was passed to allow the Trustees, all of whom were residents of the Square, to raise a rate not exceeding 2/- in the £ to pay for paving, cleansing, lighting, watching, watering and planting and to maintain the lodges at each end of Earls Terrace and the temple. They could also employ a watchman by night and an inspector by day empowered to apprehend 'malefactors, rogues, vagabonds and other disorderly persons found loitering, wandering or misbehaving themselves'.

The Trustees were equally strict with the residents, who were obliged to sweep the pavements in front of their homes every morning before 9.00am, no horses might be broken or exercised in the garden, no beasts led on the pathway and no swine allowed to roam about! Penalties were fines up to £5 or, in case of default, three months hard labour. 'Offensive residents' could be excluded from the garden, which was to be restricted to those occupying houses valued at over £30, thus excluding the grooms or coachmen living in the mews stables at the south end. In 1851 under the Kensington Improvement Act these powers were transferred to a garden committee.

GARDEN TROUBLES

The garden was the subject of prolonged controversy from 1903. The 6th Lord Kensington, who had inherited his family's financial problems, put Edwardes Square and other parts of the estate up for sale. Kensington Council considered buying the garden as an open space and the London County Council made an application to Parliament to prevent any building over it. When the sale eventually took place to private buyers, for £58,000, both proposals were dropped and although the LCC did promote the London Squares Protection Act in 1906, this applied only to those owners who were agreeable. In 1909, when the original 90-year lease from Lord Kensington was about to end the new owners lodged a claim against the Edwardes Square Garden Committee for dilapidation and in 1910 made an application to build over the garden and Earls Terrace frontage. This was refused by both the Council and LCC but in May of that year the Square residents were informed that they could no longer use these spaces and gates were locked against them in defiance of the Council's order. Council workmen were sent to unlock them.

This process occurred three times. When a resident and the beadle guarding the Square garden were manhandled the Garden Committee issued a writ against the new owners, Amalgamated Estates, which was heard on 26 July 1910, the judge finding for the residents' right to use the spaces

'for all time'. Further appeals to reverse this decision failed. On 22 January 1912 a huge celebration was held. Fifty cartloads of timber were brought in to build a 40-foot bonfire for a firework party; all the houses were lit up and a procession, led by a pipe band, circled the Square. The danger however was not entirely removed. Within a short time the freeholders proposed to build four blocks of flats on the site of Earls Terrace. This too came to naught in the face of opposition from the residents and the Terrace remained empty until 1918 when the houses were converted into flats.

In 1995 controversy returned with a plan to refurbish the whole terrace with sub-basement development under the rear gardens and an underground car park. Both residents and Council opposed but modified plans went through on appeal.

LOCAL STUDIOS

When the Horticultural Society left its nearby garden in 1824 most of its site was used as a timber yard until the southern section became Pembroke Studios. When the land was sold with the break-up of Lord Kensington's estate in 1903 the entrance to the timber yard became St Mary Abbots Place and studios were built on the east side. The first was for the sculptor, W. R. Colton, in 1910, premises that were later numbered 1 to 5. Reconstructed as film studios they have now been redeveloped as offices. Next door and built at the same time, was the studio and school of animal painting run by W. Frank Calderon, with a courtyard and kennels and 'space for a horse.' The studio and house were separated after the First World War and in 1941 the White Eagle Lodge, a religious body, took the whole building with the studio being adapted as a chapel (*see* pp. 129-130)

In its first years there was no outlet from the south side of Edwardes Square but in 1827 a way was made to the newly-built Pembroke Square. It was here in 1844 that the four Pembroke Cottages were built, only two of which remain, nos. 3 and 4 having been demolished to build Pembroke Court flats. No. 1 was the home (1879-1902) of the artist William Rothenstein and then from 1904-1919 of Laurence Housman, brother of the poet, who painted banners for the Suffragette movement in the back garden. On the opposite side of the road, The Scarsdale was built in 1866. The rest of the south side has entirely changed since. The old stables and coach houses have gone, partly replaced by studios. As on the north-east side, the corner of the square on the south-west is now a block of modern flats, an outlet to Pembroke Gardens having been made in 1860.

49. Edwardes Terrace, c.1905.

NOTABLES IN THE SQUARE

Among the many notable residents of Edwardes Square and its immediate neighbourhood were Norman O'Neill, the composer (1899-1904), and G.K. Chesterton who lived at no. 1 in the first year of his marriage, painting crayon frescos of knights and heroes on the outside back wall. Henry Justice Ford, the illustrator, lived at 5 South Edwardes Square Studios from 1894 to 1916, as did Clifford Bax, the artist and writer, from 1917 to 1925. Elizabeth Inchbald, the flamboyant novelist, dramatist and actress lodged at two addresses, one in Earls Terrace, the other in Edwardes Place, from 1816 to 1818 shortly before her death. Other residents of Earls Terrace included George du Maurier (1867-70) and Walter Pater, critic and humanist (1886-93), both at no. 12, and the poet Henry Newbolt at no. 23 from 1896 to 1907.

BUILDING ON THE HAYSTACKS

Edwardes Square was fully occupied when Lord Kensington decided to let his land to the south of it for speculative building in 1823. The 7½-acre site, bounded on the east by Earls Court Lane (Road), had until a few decades earlier been entirely rural, known as Great and Little Haystacks fields. The takers were a business partnership formed by John Dowley, who worked for the Westminster Commissioners of Sewers, and Robert Tuck, whose family building firm was also involved. No architect appears to have been employed but accounts have survived recording the sums spent not only on building materials, but foraging and farriering for the horses pulling the wagons. Both Dowling and Hunt had been engaged in the canal business and it was not long before they ran into more financial trouble with debts totalling over £10,000, one of the creditors being Lord Kensington, and many lost heavily when the pair went bankrupt in 1826.

From then on, the Pembroke development was taken over by various builders and it was 1860 before the whole square was completed. The prime contractor was William Collins, and it was to him that an 89-year lease of the central garden was granted in 1834. At its Earls Court Road end there was a lodge occupied from 1879 by a gardener called Charles Rassell. When the garden came up for auction as one of the lots in Edwardes estate sale in 1903, Rassell acquired it. In 1923 he announced his wish to build at the west end but was refused permission by the LCC. The freehold was bought by the Prudential Assurance Company for the use of the surrounding residents but Rassell was able to keep the plot at the west end for use as a tennis court and garden.

50. Pembroke Lodge.

The grandest house in the neighbourhood, Pembroke Lodge, was built in 1868 to the south of Pembroke Square, in grounds comparable in size with the square's garden. It was taken in 1909 by Andrew Bonar Law, the Conservative MP, who lived there until he went to 11 Downing Street as Chancellor of the Exchequer in 1917. It was then used as a Convalescent Home for Officers, returning to private ownership until it was demolished in 1970 to build Pembroke Gardens Close.

THE EDWARDES FAMILY

After the early failures of the 2nd Earl the financial affairs of the Edwardes family became more complicated. The 4th Earl, the 35-year-old Liberal MP for Haverford West, became Baron Kensington in the English peerage (the Edwardes were Irish title-holders). He died in 1896 and his son William Edwardes, who was 32 when he inherited, served in the Life Guards in the Boer War and died in action in 1900, just as he had raised a huge loan.

The title and estate went to his brother who, faced with these enormous financial commitments, decided to sell the whole estate. There was no precedent for a sale of such magnitude, said the *Daily Telegraph*. It took place in two parts. In the first, the area south of Pembroke Road, the buyer was Edward Guinness, Baron Iveagh, for £565,000. The second sale a few months later, in November 1903, saw the land divided into smaller lots, the largest holdings going to the Prudential Assurance Company

LEAFY LEXHAM

Despite the small leafy enclosure at its eastern end, Lexham Gardens can hardly be considered a 'Square'. One of the later developments on the portion of the Edwardes estate to the east of the Earls Court Road, its creation resulted from an agreement in 1866 between William Edwardes, the 3rd Lord Kensington, and two other local land-owners, Robert Gunter and Henry Alexander, to co-operate in the extension of Cromwell Road from Gloucester Road, where it petered out, to Earls Court Road.

Lexham Road, as it was originally called, was part of a scheme to provide a through way from Kensington High Street to Cromwell Road. The change to 'Gardens' came in 1878 when the communal garden was added to the plan between the two rows of houses on the northern side of the street where it swung towards the Earls Court Road.

Many of the best-known builders of the day showed interest and during the next decade many more joined in. The houses were very grand, Italianate style with Doric–pillared porticoes and terraced balconies, intended for upper middle-class families with three or four servants living-in. The development almost immediately attracted Army officers, both active and retired. One of the most prosperous, a 35-year-old captain in the Royal Engineers, the head of a household canvassed in the 1881 census, had nine servants including a footman, butler and two nurses to look after a family of six.

The strongly represented Indian Army was headed by Sir Henry Norman, later a Governor of Queensland. Among civilian professionals were a number of doctors, barristers and clergyman. The barristers included Sydney Woolf, whose son, Leonard, recalled his childhood at 101 Lexham Gardens in the 1880s. He would be sent to Lexham Gardens Mews to tell the coachman, Dennis, at what time he would be needed to drive his father to King's Bench Walk in the brougham. This mews was only part of the maze of stables and 'walks' in which the area abounds to accommodate the vehicles, horses and drivers of the affluent Vic-

51. Lexham Gardens, c.1905.

torian occupants, and which in modern times have become desirable residences in their own right. These include Lexham Mews and Radley Mews at the west end, Pennant Mews, leading into Marloes Road, Cornwall Gardens Walk ('Stables' until 1948) and Lexham Walk. The latter provided access on foot from Lexham to Cornwall Gardens the result of pressure from the Vestry in 1887.

The new fashion for mansion flats or 'chambers' was resisted here until the 1880s. In 1887, Huntingdon House, converted during the course of construction, was the first, designed by Richard Norman Shaw. Moscow Mansions, in brilliant red brick, followed in 1891, next to Tower House on the corner of Earls Court and Cromwell Roads which includes among its past residents the impresario Imry Kiralfy of White City, Olympia and Earls Court Exhibition fame, and is now the headquarters of LAMDA

Although small compared to its neighbours, Edwardes and Pembroke, the refurbished garden enclosure of Lexham Gardens is cherished by the residents and has won several awards in garden contests.

THE MILITARY VILLAGE

The larger central reservation of Cornwall Gardens also lacks the intimacy that is provided by a surround of smaller dwellings, particularly now that almost all the grand houses have been broken up into flats. This development, a venture of the younger members of the piano-making Broadwood family, owners of the land from the early nineteenth century, was earlier than Lexham, with sewers being laid in 1862 for the parallel roads with a central garden. First choice of name was 'Gloucester' but this was changed to 'Cornwall' to mark the 21st birthday of the Prince of Wales, Duke of Cornwall (later Edward VII).

This neighbourhood also attracted the military, in particular the Indian Army and soon became known as Maine's Village Community, based on the social structure of the British Raj in Northern India. Between 1880 and 1900 its list of residents reads like a Who's Who of these expatriates, numerous members of the Council of India, judges, high ranking Army Officers, an Inspector General of Hospitals and many other administrators. The arts were thinly represented but did include, at no. 18, Sir James Scott, the Army historian, and his novelist wife, Lady Harriet Scott and the sculptor Sir James Edgar Boehm, at no. 78.

It had originally been hoped to build a church at the western end of Cornwall Gardens which had already been blocked off by the building of the new workhouse (St Mary Abbots Hospital). In 1864 the construction of the Metropolitan and District Railway aggravated the situation as the 'cut and cover' excavations sterilised a wide strip of land right across the end of the central garden and the roadway. By the time it had been filled in and reconveyed to William Broadwood the principal builder in the Gardens was William Willett senior, whose son of the same name was to become the pioneer of 'Daylight Saving'. Standards were high and strictly adhered to: every one of the grand houses had to be worth at least £2,500 to £3,500 and have three water closets as well as many other amenities, refinements and opulent décor. It was Willett who in 1877 built the eight grandiose buildings known as Cornwall Mansions of which Garden and Cornwall Houses were the most sumptuous, with 50-foot dining rooms, billiard salons and boudoirs. The six houses behind were only slightly smaller and less splendid. Terence Rattigan, the playwright, was born in one of these, no. 3, known as Lanarkslea, in 1911, when it was the home of his grandfather a Chief Justice of the Punjab.

Between the wars all these houses were converted into flats. Nos. 4, 6 & 8 became Braemar Mansions, where Ivy Compton Burnett, the author, and Margaret Jordan, the decorative arts expert, shared a flat from 1934 for many years. Willett's other houses on the north and south sides of the garden enclosure attracted many distinguished residents. *The Gentlewoman*, a fashionable periodical, described one of the houses, no. 46, in glowing detail. It belonged at that time to the 3rd Lord Abinger but was demolished in 1932 to build

52. *Cornwall Mansions, looking east. An early and sumptuous apartment building to which the description 'Mansions' really applied.*

the modern block, Stanford Court. Cornwall Gardens also had generous provision of mews stables built behind the north side (Kynance Mews) and on the south side, Cornwall Mews, which straddles Grenville Place.

QUEENS GATE GARDENS

The Thurloe/Alexander family that owned the estate which bears their name is said to have acquired it in the seventeenth century as a gift from Oliver Cromwell to their ancestor, his Secretary of State, John Thurloe (1616-1668). More prosaically it was probably acquired through an 18th-century marriage. By 1713 the scattered fields belonged to Thurloe's grandson and it was not until 1826, in the lifetime of a much later descendant, that building began on the land. In 1860, through the initiative of Henry Brown Alexander, one of these piecemeal properties, an area of about 14½ acres on the east side of the present Gloucester Road, was about to become Queens Gate Gardens.

All was busy round about with the development of the huge area acquired by the Commissioners of the Great Exhibition and the Harrington estate. Alexander was as active as any of his neighbours and used some of their work people and advisors, such as the builder-developer, Charles Aldin. The grandson of an Uxbridge carpenter, Aldin, who had worked for Cubitt in Pimlico, was to be responsible, with his son who succeeded him, for building over 200 houses and about as many mews stables and cottages in this area.

Alexander granted Aldin 99-year building leases on the three fields, the plan being for 127 houses and 51 stables over a period of approximately twelve years. The central garden square, unlike most of those made earlier, followed a new pattern with some houses opening directly on the garden without a dividing carriageway. This applied to ten early houses on the Gloucester Road frontage, which were knocked down in recent times to build Campbell Court. Among the first residents were two members of the Outram family (the offspring of the Duke of Clarence, later William IV, and the actress Mrs Jordan), Sir James Outram and the Earl of Munster. Other houses had equally upper-class occupants, as was intended from the start. These included two wealthy brewer-landowners, Samuel Whitbread and Edward Charrington, an American banker, Hugh McCulloch, the proprietors of the *Manchester Guardian*, the barrister John E. Taylor and the Earl of Strathmore. Most of the heads of households, their children varying from eight or nine to a modest two, were middle-aged and the average number of servants was eight or nine.

In common with builders and developers everywhere those involved in the creation of Queens Gate Gardens had constant financial problems. Aldin had an extra disadvantage as he was also responsible for all the roads and sewers and the garden layout, which on adjoining sites the Commissioners for the Exhibition had provided at their own expense. In 1865 it was estimated that the houses would let at rents of £350 per annum. If Aldin has been forgotten by all except serious students of Victorian architecture, he has a quaint memorial in the flue arches that are characteristic of the Queens Gate area and are only fully appreciated in aerial photographs. The ornamental arches, like flying buttresses, carry the flues from the lower Mews' chimneys (which would have polluted the first floors of their high-class neighbours) up the rear of the great houses that back on to them.

53. The drawing room of 30 Queens Gate Gardens in 1896.

54. *The north side of Kensington High Street before shops were built upon the front gardens.*

The High Street

EARLY DAYS

When Leigh Hunt wrote 'The Old Court Suburb' as the first of a series of vignettes for *Household Words* in 1835, his view of Kensington was far from glowing. He described its streets as 'often … dreary, monotonous and barrack-like'. His 'suburb' did not include the villages of Notting Hill, Earls Court or Brompton, but was merely the cluster of buildings around the old parish church of St Mary Abbots and the Palace which Dutch William and Mary, daughter of the deposed James II, had made from the country mansion, Nottingham House, a century and half earlier. This was still hardly more than a village which straggled along a narrow High Street, and was starting to encroach up the southern slope of Campden Hill and touching streets with the neighbouring Earls Court, where cattle still grazed in the fields.

Before the arrival of the royal inhabitants Kensington had been a village one passed through leaving London westward, a place to visit rather than to live. Samuel Pepys wrote of 'an evening's sport' there, although he did not specify the hostelry. It could well have been the Red Lion, one of the oldest and largest inns, situated roughly in the area opposite Old Court Place.

Those who complain today about changes in pub names may be surprised to learn that the practice was rife long ago and there are few better examples than Kensington's old High Street. Here,

in a very short distance on the south side, over twenty inns existed over a period of two hundred or so years and many changed their names two or even three times. A happy exception is the surviving Goat, established *c.*1695, although altered and refurbished in Victorian times.

It was only the short length of the highway between the Goat and the Adam & Eve, on the corner of a mews of that name, that was known as the High Street until comparatively modern times, the rest being the Kensington Road from Knightsbridge to Hammersmith. By the time the royal family moved into their Kensington palace in the spring of 1690 a string of small shops had appeared on the south side of the High Street near the Goat, opposite the main gate and what is now Palace Avenue. Of these the shells of five buildings still remain – nos. 17 to 25 (odd), squeezed between their much later neighbours.

The first spate of building included several high-class houses, one of which replaced the Red Lion, and some smaller dwellings, all of which were to be converted with shops on their ground floors as time went by. Two or three of these actually remained until the coming of the railway in the 1860s. But as the tradespeople arrived, within ten years most of the frontage between the Goat and what is now Derry Street filled up. At least one slum court was established in the land behind them, the beginnings of a 'rookery' which was to proliferate in Victorian days (*see* pp. 136-137).

In 1854 *The Kensington Gazette* reported that 'Kensington High Street was rapidly improving. Several old buildings have been replaced by new

55. The south side of Kensington High Street, between The Goat and Kensington Court, c.1905.

and handsome houses while the mean and narrow fronts of many shops are giving way to glass and brass, showing their change by night by a cheerful illumination of gas. Mr. Brassington, the bookseller, has reared a creditable exterior, Mr. Ball, the bootmaker, by throwing two houses into one, has presented a trading mart inferior to few in the metropolis and Mr. Colbourne, by boldly making three premises into one in his drapery establishment, has produced a frontage rivalling any similar emporium in Regent Street.'

Amongst these a significant name also appeared, that of James Toms, who had a grocery shop just east of Young Street for about fifteen years from 1824. He is believed to have been related, possibly the father, to Joseph Toms who opened a toy and fancy repository a few doors away in 1836 which was to lead eventually to the family's part in the great High Street selling revolution. (*See* pp. 68-69).

However, in 1851 Leigh Hunt was complaining about the traffic when travelling from Kensington to the City, 'What with waiting for an omnibus and its stoppages when I got in, I found myself at a quarter to four just arrived at Knightsbridge when I ought to have been at Temple Bar.' This

is in contrast to Thackeray's joy some six years earlier at the provision of omnibuses every two minutes near his home in Young Street. 'What can a mortal want more?' he wrote to his mother.

ROAD WIDENING

In Leigh Hunt's time the High Street was still very narrow and winding, the footpaths poor, the lighting almost non-existent. The Vestry knew something had to be done. There was also talk of the new underground railway and the rebuilding of the parish church. In 1861 a serious fire removed some of the older buildings opposite the junction with Church Street, enabling the dangerous curve in the road there to be cut back by about sixty feet. In 1864 a Vestry committee asked the Metropolitan Board of Works, the body responsible for major works in London, to carry out an improvement to the High Street 'which has now become the main western line of thoroughfare out of London, where often times fatal accidents occur and serious blocks to the traffic nearly hourly take place.'

The Board agreed and the Improvement Act of 1866 allowed the whole of the south side of the High Street to be set back and a new road, Ball Street, named after the Chairman of the Vestry

56. *A view of Kensington High Street looking westwards to St Mary Abbots in 1897. The photographer was standing by the entrance to Kensington Palace opposite The Goat public house. The decorations are to celebrate Queen Victoria's Diamond Jubilee. The pub on the right is the Kings Arms.*

Committee, Edward Ball, built at the rear. The new frontage was to be occupied entirely by shops with three or four storeys above their plate glass windows. Only two pubs were built, a new Duke of Sussex replacing the 1785 building (originally the Three Compasses) and the Duke of Abercorn, renamed the Town Hall Tavern in 1871.

In 1870 *The Kensington News* announced that there were now '55 superb newly-built shops on the south side of the High Street'. One of them, described as 'a handsome large shop property with plate glass front, three floors of rooms and lofty basement' had been taken by Mr John Barker, who was to have a profound affect on the whole of the area's commercial and civic life for many decades to come.

It is surprising that Francis Tucker's candle factory, founded in 1765, survived until 1900 only yards behind this terrace of new shops on a large site east of High Street, Kensington station, belching out greasy black smoke (*see* pp. 72-73).

For the last thirty years of the nineteenth century the names of Barker, Ponting, Derry and Toms, shuffled the shop fronts like a pack of cards with only a few once-flourishing smaller businesses holding out against them. One of the conditions of the 1866 Improvement Act was that freeholds would have to be sold after ten years, although long leases were offered. This happened in 1873 when several were bought by the Crown, adding a strong official voice to future developments on both sides of the High Street well into the twentieth century. Between The Goat and Young Street as leases ended and rebuilding took place in late Victorian times, banks and larger shops began to take over from the smaller traders. Notable among the latter were Budgens, Keith Prowse Ticket Office Piano and Music shop, and Slater's butchers and fishmongers, which later moved across the road next to the newly-built Royal Palace Hotel. On the corner of Young Street, Story's furnishing business, occupying three large shops, flourished from 1900 to its destruction by fire in 1947. After a brief spell as a branch of Hamptons, the building was reconstructed and is now mainly occupied by the Kensington Market.

Although less-developed in its earliest days, the north side of the High Street, from the boundary of the Palace grounds to some 300 yards west of the church, was not slow to catch up, with shops and a generous supply of public houses from the Kings Arms to the Civet Cat and the Crown on either corner of Church Street. Joseph Addison, and later William Thackeray, both patronised the Kings Arms on the corner of Palace Avenue and Thackeray set the climax of *Henry Esmond* there. The Civet Cat ceased being an inn in 1900 but its

57.   Kensington High Street between Kensington Court and Young Street in 1909, when expiration of leases was causing many changes.   Some businesses survived into the 1960s including Keith Prowse (right).

sign has remained over a bank and a restaurant; the Crown changed to retail use in the 1970s.

In 1841 the Crown Commissioners decided to construct the new Queens Road, now Kensington Palace Gardens, across the kitchen gardens of the Palace from Bayswater to the High Street in Kensington. They bought a small site there, consisting of two houses and the Grapes public house, to provide its southern entrance, but the maze of courts and lanes behind the rest of the frontage was unaffected. Here were Clarence Place and Cousins Terrace and Brown's Buildings, the alley-way where the little Royal Kent Theatre (see pp. 145-146) existed for a few years from 1831.

Old photographs show a crowded shopping terrace where a variety of traders provided services and goods from photographic studios to provision stores, stationers, florists, fishmongers and silversmiths. The whole of this side of the High Street was demolished for road widening in 1903 and advertised as a building site by the Crown Commissioners but there were no buyers, despite early suggestions for a cinema. Most of the site was eventually taken by Barker's. Among the old shops here were a number that proudly advertised

58.   The Civet Cat before rebuilding in 1902. It stood on the south-east corner of Church Street.

59. The south side of Kensington High Street in 1912. The picture shows an extension to Derry and Toms which took over the old Town Hall Tavern, a ubiquitous Lyons teashop, and some brands of cigarettes of the past - State Express and Abdulla.

their royal warrants such as the linen-drapers Breeze and James at no. 32, established in 1810, who went as far as changing their name to Coburg House when the young Victoria married Prince Albert.

YESTERDAY'S SHOPS

Between St Mary Abbots Church and the old school and Vestry Hall, and later the Town Hall, a short terrace of shops remains, but vastly different in character to how it was before the 1st World War. Then it included an undertaker, Betts the Butchers and Parr's, later the Westminster and then National Westminster Bank, which has recently been relinquished to retail use. Similarly, the shops further west illuminate the social history of nearly a century ago: the Aerated Bread Company (ABC) tea shop, Dr Jaeger's Sanitary Woollen System, forerunner of the famous fashion name, and beneath Hornton Court, which replaced half of Lower Phillimore Place in 1905, a Turkish baths, Daniel Neal's, famous for children's shoes and school uniforms, Cramer's music shop, founded by the composer and musician, Johann Baptist Cramer and a Mudie's Select Library.

The second half of Lower Phillimore Place,

between Campden Hill Road and Argyll Road, had already succumbed to commerce by the conversion of its ground floors into shops and its front gardens were replaced by a terraced pavement. This terrace was the first building speculation of William Phillimore, who in 1779 had inherited the 64 acres of land north of the main road, originally part of the Campden House estate. He was the great-grandson of the merchant who had acquired it in the early years of the century. It was his descendants who would eventually fill the fields climbing the hill with terraces of handsome houses such as those in Stafford Terrace, Essex Villas and Upper Phillimore Gardens, as well as several larger villas.

Until replaced by the modern flats Stafford, Phillimore and Troy Courts in the 1930s, the rest of the terrace remained as it had been built between 1788 and 1813, a row of three-storey houses, the frontages of which were decorated with carved swathes of drapery, giving them the nick-name 'dishclout row'. Their gardens, with railed walls and a row of large trees, separated them from the bustle of the main road.

The lodge houses and gate to Holland Park and the parkland wall took up the long frontage of the High Street from the end of Upper Phillimore Place to Melbury Road. The lodges were demolished with the widening of the road and the building of the Commonwealth Institute (*see* p. 81) in 1960. Melbury Court had occupied the rest of the site in 1928, although the golf school behind survived into the 1930s.

When their old dairy was knocked down with other farm buildings the Tonks, tenants of Holland Farm, were allowed to put up a new dairy on a small site between Melbury Road and Holland Lane. Here cows were still being milked in the early years of this century. The shop was later taken over by United Dairies. The Holland Arms replaced the ancient White Horse in 1866, in a terrace of shops, Holland Place, which included the Kensington Wheeling Centre selling bicycles.

St Mary Abbots Terrace was the first of the third Lord Holland's building ventures in 1824. Extending from Russell Road to Melbury Road, it consisted of about twenty pairs of houses with large, tree-lined front gardens. Behind them was a mews which between 1920 and its demise became an artists' colony as did the south side of Holland Park Road.

The St Mary Abbots Terrace redevelopment put the backs of the houses on to the main road, hidden behind a high wall. Flats, shops, offices and the Royal Kensington, now Olympia Hilton, Hotel occupied the western section.

Key to Buildings Around Kensington High Street 1700-1900

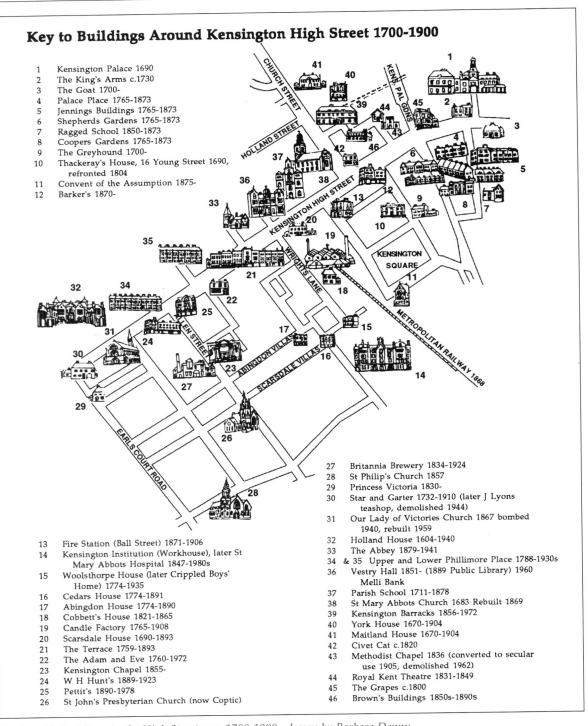

1   Kensington Palace 1690
2   The King's Arms c.1730
3   The Goat 1700-
4   Palace Place 1765-1873
5   Jennings Buildings 1765-1873
6   Shepherds Gardens 1765-1873
7   Ragged School 1850-1873
8   Coopers Gardens 1765-1873
9   The Greyhound 1700-
10 Thackeray's House, 16 Young Street 1690,
      refronted 1804
11 Convent of the Assumption 1875-
12 Barker's 1870-

13 Fire Station (Ball Street) 1871-1906
14 Kensington Institution (Workhouse), later St
      Mary Abbots Hospital 1847-1980s
15 Woolsthorpe House (later Crippled Boys'
      Home) 1774-1935
16 Cedars House 1774-1891
17 Abingdon House 1774-1890
18 Cobbett's House 1821-1865
19 Candle Factory 1765-1908
20 Scarsdale House 1690-1893
21 The Terrace 1759-1893
22 The Adam and Eve 1760-1972
23 Kensington Chapel 1855-
24 W H Hunt's 1889-1923
25 Pettit's 1890-1978
26 St John's Presbyterian Church (now Coptic)

27 Britannia Brewery 1834-1924
28 St Philip's Church 1857
29 Princess Victoria 1830-
30 Star and Garter 1732-1910 (later J Lyons
      teashop, demolished 1944)
31 Our Lady of Victories Church 1867 bombed
      1940, rebuilt 1959
32 Holland House 1604-1940
33 The Abbey 1879-1941
34 & 35 Upper and Lower Phillimore Place 1788-1930s
36 Vestry Hall 1851- (1889 Public Library) 1960
      Melli Bank
37 Parish School 1711-1878
38 St Mary Abbots Church 1683 Rebuilt 1869
39 Kensington Barracks 1856-1972
40 York House 1670-1904
41 Maitland House 1670-1904
42 Civet Cat c.1820
43 Methodist Chapel 1836 (converted to secular
      use 1905, demolished 1962)
44 Royal Kent Theatre 1831-1849
45 The Grapes c.1800
46 Brown's Buildings 1850s-1890s

60. Notable buildings in the High Street area 1700-1900; drawn by Barbara Denny.

61. *The corner of Earls Court Road and Kensington High Street c.1960. The most enduring 'bomb site', it was not redeveloped until the 1980s. This was the site of the 18th-century Star & Garter Tavern.*

62. *Lower Phillimore Place, showing the stretch from Hornton Street to Campden Hill Road.*

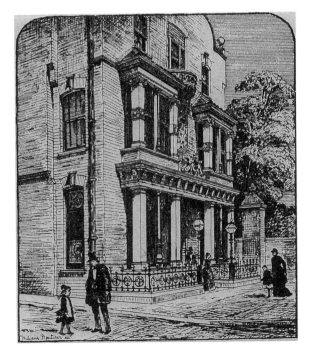

63. (Top left) Advertisement in 1909 for C.E. Betts, family butcher of 86 Kensington High Street. 'Purveyor of the finest Scotch Beef and Mutton; fine pickled tongues and Dairy-fed Pork.'

64. (Bottom left) The Holland Park Dairy run by Tunks & Tisdall. From The Building News, 12 April 1878.

65. The White Horse in Kensington High Street. This 19th-century engraving notes that it was 'Remarkable only as the Traditionary retreat of Addison after his unfortunate Marriage with the Countess of Warwick'.

SCARSDALE HOUSE

On the south side of the High Street the land immediately west of Wrights Lane was known as Browman's Field. This 15-acre plot is now covered by Iverna and Cheniston Gardens and Scarsdale Place, the latter named after a 17th-century villa called Scarsdale House which was eventually swallowed up by the Pontings' store in the 1920s. It stood behind a high wall in four acres of garden that included a 'canal' and a fishpond. It was built *c*.1690 by City mercer, Francis Barry, who like his neighbour, Thomas Young, in Kensington Square, was an early property speculator. Too ambitious, he over-reached himself and within ten years most of the land was sold off to pay his creditors and he was forced to move to a more modest home.

The new owner was another mercer whose son and heir eventually sold off a large portion of the estate to a clergyman, Dr Samuel Clarke, and his friend Sir Isaac Newton, who never lived there but intended the property to benefit a niece who was caring for him in his old age. His intentions were thwarted by her daughter whose financial difficulties resulted in its sale to a stablekeeper and coachmaker, Gregory Wright, in 1753. It was he who gave his name to the lane when he built along it what he described as a 'few villas'. These were Woolsthorpe House, honouring Newton whose birthplace was Woolsthorpe in Lincolnshire, Abingdon House, Scarsdale Lodge and Cedar Villa.

In its early years, Scarsdale House included among its residents the Duchess of Monmouth, widow of the rebel Duke, a Lord Mayor of London in 1697, the wool merchant, Sir Humphrey Edwin and several other folk high in the society of their times. The Curzon family took its freehold in 1720 and it was from the title of the later Curzons' peerage that it got its name in 1761, although no family members lived there then and it was used as a school.

The temptation of rising land prices must have proved too much for the lawyer who took its long lease in 1783 and within five years the stables to the north of the house had become a row of houses. By 1825 the garden was covered by Scarsdale Terrace along the east side of Wrights Lane.

However, the house itself was enlarged and refurbished by Edward Cecil Curzon, a wealthy antiquarian, but the encroachment of the railway and commercial expansion could not be halted. In the 1890s it was acquired by Pontings, and remnants of the house were incorporated later into a 'tea and retiring room for ladies.'

In the midst of all this change and destruction the stalwart radical, William Cobbett, had set out on his 'Rural Rides' from a cottage behind Scarsdale House in the 1820s (*see* p.118).

Before his financial collapse, Francis Barry had begun to raise money on his Browman's Field by dividing the main road frontage into strips to let on building leases from 1760. The nine houses of what became The Terrace were of varied appearance but all were charming and survived until the end of the nineteenth century. In their early days they would have been regarded as a pleasant suburban development on the outskirts of the town, for after the Adam & Eve there were only scattered houses until one reached Hammersmith.

In 1772 one of the houses was described as 'being lately in the occupation of the Countess Findlater, with six very good bedrooms and a large walled garden planted with the choicest fruit trees and shrubs.' All The Terrace gardens were lengthy and covered the whole site of the present Iverna Court and Gardens. Residents at various times included George Davys, Dean of Chester and tutor to Princess Victoria; Henry Cole, the key figure in the development of 'Museumland'; William Banting, an upholsterer by trade who ironically became famous for his work on corpulence, which gave rise to the use of his name for dieting, and John Leech, the *Punch* artist.

In 1866 the prosperous High Street cheesemonger and Vestryman, Jubal Webb, moved into no. 2. In 1893, when the leases expired he bought the freehold and proceeded to replace The Terrace with a row of shops known as The Promenade, flanked at the rear by Iverna Gardens and Court, although for a while Webb flirted with a scheme to build a concert and exhibition hall.

The blocks of flats were erected between 1898 and 1903 and advertised as being 'replete with every modern convenience, including telephones, messenger boxes, passenger and tradesmen's lifts, electric light and liveried attendants.' There was also the assurance that the flats would be occupied 'at good fair rentals, none less than £180 per annum, by people in excellent positions' and 'there was not the slightest vestige of possibility of their ever becoming tenanted by artisans or the working classes.' The central garden was to have a fountain, rockery and shrubbery but this did not materialise for some years. In more recent times the residents themselves arranged a more attractive layout.

The L-shaped Cheniston Gardens replaced Abingdon House in 1879, early residents of which included Sydney Ponting, who also lodged some of his assistants there. The Cedar Villa site was sold in 1891 to a local builder who put up the five blocks of flats in Marloes Road, Cedar, Zetland, Rutland, Falkland and Sutherland Houses, while Woolsthorpe House, sold in 1935, was demolished to build Kensington Close Hotel. This was origi-

66. *The Terrace as it appeared c.1850 (Kensington High Street between Wrights Lane and Adam and Eve Mews).*

nally a block of service flats run on residential club lines. The London Tara Hotel next door, built in 1971-73 with a large government subsidy to encourage business with Ireland, stands on the old coal yard land. The site had first been considered by the LCC as one for a 26-storey tower block but this was thrown out after a public outcry.

THE TAILOR'S LANDS

The Adam & Eve pub at 163 Kensington High Street originally stood in a large garden and when it was put up for auction in 1765 was said 'to have a delightful view towards Holland House and from the rear, a prospect to Surrey.' It was rebuilt in 1823 and absorbed into the new frontage in 1882, at about the time the row of cottages behind was being changed into a mews and some of the stables used to house police horses. The Middlesex Rifles also had a drill hall here. In Edwardian days Kensington's first cinema, The Royalty with a narrow entrance-foyer in the High Street, now no. 177, extended back into the mews, remained until the Second World War and served tea and biscuits, included in the ticket price, to its matinee audiences.

The mews suffered severe damage early in 1940 when a bomb destroyed the cinema together with Long's Buildings, a 19th-century stable block converted into small dwellings. The site remained vacant or used as a car park until the building of houses in 1985.

Complicated questions of ownership prevented the development of the Kensington Road's southern side from the official end of the High Street at the Adam & Eve. After a case in Chancery in 1801 the large site of over ten acres was split up and sold to various developers. The most prominent of these was Thomas Allen, a tailor and breeches maker of Old Bond Street, who is said

to have made most of his very considerable fortune supplying uniforms during the Napoleonic Wars. His son, Thomas Newland Allen, named for one of his father's country estates, and the Allen family, were associated with this part of Kensington for well over a century. After the fashion of the time their developments on the main road were divided into terraces, Somerset Terrace, Bath Place, Allen and Newland Terraces and Newland Place, up to the corner of Earls Court Road, and the Star & Garter pub.

67. *The Adam & Eve, closed in 1972.*

All the houses were fairly large, set back from the road, with long gardens behind and in their early days attracted good class residents. Allen's solicitor William à Beckett, who is believed to have been the model for Dickens's Ralph Nickleby, was quick tempered and quarrelsome. Thomas Faulkner, the contemporary historian, did not like the new houses, describing them as 'covered with plaister' (plaster or stucco), 'a tasteless innovation' compared to brick, he said. In the 1870s, as the old leases began to fall in, ground floor shops replaced the front gardens. The freeholds of the first two terraces, between the Mews and Allen Street, remained with the Phillimore family. Frank Chesterton of the same family as GK, and the Phillimores' long-standing estate agents, redeveloped these for them in 1908 to his own designs. From 1890 this terrace included the well known drapers Pettit's (*see* pp. 71-72).

At the same time, Allen House, a block of very large mansion flats, was built behind the old Bath Place on the east side of Allen Street. In the 1980s this became one of the area's first 'time-share' blocks, the flats multiplied by sub-division, a controversial development that engendered much anxiety.

In his earliest days of ownership, the first Thomas Allen had formed two streets southwards, first Newland Street (now Abingdon Road), followed shortly after by Allen Street. The latter remained a cul-de-sac until long after his death and little building took place until the twelve houses in Phillimore Place in 1843. It was here that Leigh Hunt lived briefly at no. 2, 1851-2, before departing broken-hearted to Hammersmith following the death of his favourite son, Vincent. The house was later occupied by Baroness Orczy, of *Scarlet Pimpernel* fame, and her husband, Montague Barstow, who had a photographic studio in the garden. Later it was the home of Rachel Ferguson, who wrote several well-known books on the area

before and after the Second World War, including *Passionate Kensington*.

This High Street hinterland included the Britannia Brewery on the west side of Allen Street opposite Kensington Chapel, and of which now only the Britannia pub remains, the brewery being replaced by Allen Mansions in 1928.

W. H. Hunt, a drapery department store that occupied almost half the block, dominated the High Street frontage between Allen Street and Abingdon Road between 1889 and 1923. In 1919 Barker's, who wished to expand, offered £40,000 for it but were refused; but it succumbed to redevelopment when a Woolworth's store was built here in 1923, although the two corner premises, nos. 197-9, still retain a vestige of their 19th-century structure.

A much earlier block of flats (1883), was that of Wynnstay Gardens, behind Allen Terrace, intended at first to be a row of houses. Among its early residents was the sculptor, Sir William Hamo Thornycroft (1884-1991). When the Roman Catholic Church of Our Lady of Victories was built in 1867, standing back from the main frontage there was a gap of barely 33 feet between the shops through which it could be seen and this remains despite its rebuilding after war-time destruction. An early 19th-century cottage latterly occupied by the building firm of Walter Nash, remained until this time as did cow sheds.

The Star & Garter, on the corner of Earls Court Road, was an eighteenth-century tavern rebuilt in Victorian times. This was closed in 1910 and the site used for a large Lyons tea shop until 1944 when a flying bomb destroyed this and adjacent buildings with many casualties. This remained the most enduring bomb site in the borough as debates raged as to its future. It was redeveloped with shops, offices and flats in the 1980s. The Princess Victoria, built in 1860, is all that is left of old times in this stretch.

The short distance of the Kensington Road's southern side from Earls Court Road to Earls Terrace was part of the same development as that of Edwardes Square in 1815 and had the same financial ups and downs. It consisted of sixteen houses called Leonard Row (Place) none of which now survives. First to go was the corner of Earls Court Road, in 1874 when six new houses and shops were built, the two facing the High Street being taken by the London & Westminster Bank and redeveloped in the 1920s for the Midland. Also in 1874/5 the next houses in Leonard Place became a 'carriage manufactory', Henry Whitlock Ltd, succeeded by another 'high class coach builders' Strachan and Brown. As times changed, the Century Motor Co. Ltd took over with a 'garage

68. *The Britannia Brewery in Allen Street, c.1926, prior to its demolition. The Britannia pub on the right survives.*

for 150 cars' at the back, advertising Astahl Touring Cars, Berna Commercial Motors and Aster chassis and spares. The site was to become an 'aircraft factory' and an amusement park before its later final use as a Post Office. Next door the Kensington Kinema, the 'largest in the country' with seating for 2,350 people, was opened in 1926. The building, which has now been converted into six smaller cinemas, then included a restaurant and a large billiard saloon. Its name was changed to the Majestic, then to The Kensington, and is now the Odeon. The present shops and flats, Leonards Court, replaced the remainder of Leonard Place in 1930.

THE HOUSES IN BETWEEN

At about the same time as the first widening of Kensington High Street a partnership between a young member of a wealthy farming family and a bank, later to be part of National Westminster, produced a scheme to fill the 18 acres of orchards

and pastures, known as Watts Field, with profitable streets.

In 1810 land had been enfranchised to Samuel Hutchings of Earls Court Farm and when Hutchings died in 1844, William Nokes, a member of a farming family in Upminster, approached his widow, Sarah, with a view to purchasing the fields with a £11,000 loan. This was fairly straightforward but from then the financial arrangements became much more complicated with the participation of a number of other interested parties.

At this time the London and County Bank itself became involved and it was one of its directors, James Rhodes, who finally took over the development and the selling of building leases. Among the first buildings in Marloes Road was the Devonshire Arms, *c.*1850, which had a 'club room on the first floor, two parlours, a skittle ground with a carpenter's shop over it and a large bowling green.' The builder was a Richard Anderson who had leased a nearby brickfield of 27½ acres for

£450 a year, plus a royalty of six shillings for every thousand bricks over four million made in a year. He was engaged in a number of other ventures in the vicinity before he went bankrupt in 1853.

Despite difficulties there was steady progress in the building of streets such as Abingdon Road and Villas, Inkerman Terrace, Cope Place, Scarsdale Villas and the eastern side of Earls Court Road. Even the suicide of the bank's chairman, John Sadlier, caused little more than a hiatus in 1856.

No churches had been planned in the original development scheme but this was remedied by the conveyance of a site for St Philip's in 1856 and the Scots Presbyterian, St John's, in Scarsdale Villas in 1862, now St Marks Coptic Church. (*See* p.128)

Over 23 builders had been involved. The families, who moved in were a mixture of middle class and lower paid professionals and tradesmen such as piano makers, probably employed at the Erards factory in Warwick Road. There were also a few artists and sculptors and in the 1890s more of these were attracted to Scarsdale Studios off Stratford Road.

Only Blithfield Street in the south-east corner of the estate seems to have been built specifically for working-class occupation, namely the workmen rendered homeless by the Metropolitan Board of Works improvements around the High Street and the building of the railway in 1869. The early occupants of seventeen small houses numbered no less than 176 people, including over twenty children under two years old. A century later these same houses, prettily painted, some round a courtyard garden, were being eulogised by estate agents and sold for sums which would have kept those Victorian families in luxury for the whole of their lives.

The fashion for large mansion flats in the 1890s had a considerable influence on the area between Kensington High Street and Cromwell Road.

69. *Mr Bethel and Mr Richardson, two of the directors of the Kensington builders, Walter Nash. They are outside their head office, a 19th-century cottage demolished in the 1960s for the rebuilding of Our Lady of Victories church and the corner of Earls Court Road.*

Abingdon Court and Abingdon Gardens were both completed in the first years of this century. The former had hydraulic lifts installed, powered by the London Hydraulic Power Company which had an 184-mile network of pipes under London. The company closed in 1971 and the lifts were converted to electric power and eventually replaced by new elevators.

Kings of Commerce

THE BARKER EMPIRE

The young John Barker was eleven when his parents brought him to London to visit the Great Exhibition. Perhaps it was that which set his mind against following his father's trade as a brewer in Maidstone. He chose instead to be apprenticed to a draper.

After some minor posts he came to London and by the mid 1860s he was working for William Whiteley in Westbourne Grove, becoming departmental manager at a salary of £300 a year. But, when he sought a partnership, Whiteley refused, although offering him a large salary increase to £1000 a year. It was then that with the financial backing of a wealthy Bradford merchant, James Whitehead, he raised enough capital to take two of the new shops just built on the south side of Kensington's High Street. By the end of the first year of business he was already expanding, not only in the High Street but also in Ball Street at the rear, where later there were complaints about the encroachment of his carts and vans. He and his family lived over the shops, with servants and eight female assistants, three milliners, two salesmen and a porter. As the premises proliferated so did the functions they served until there was hardly a household need ignored. As well as the drapery, there was men's tailoring, book-selling, stationery, ironmongery, groceries and provisions, wines and spirits, furnishings, furniture and carpets. In 1887 the magazine *The Queen* dubbed Barker's 'the best establishment in London for moderate prices.' In twenty years or so he had twenty-eight shops in Kensington, a staff of over 1,000 and a delivery service with eighty horses. In 1884 Barker and Whitehead fell out and Tresham Gilbey, who had married Barker's daughter Ann, bought Whitehead out. With Barker as its first chairman, the firm became a limited company.

More expansion followed with the erection of an imposing building on the corner of Young Street which housed a food hall and carpet department. The firm also had its own building department and houses in Kensington Square for live-in staff. In 1895 a furniture depository was opened on the old Erard factory site in Cromwell Crescent. This was enlarged and a block of flats, Warwick Mansions, built on one side. With the whole High Street frontage taken up between Young and Derry Streets the John Barker tentacles stretched across to the north side where in 1902-5 a building was erected to house the furniture and other new departments. Profits

70. *John Barker.*

soared and in 1906, the year the firm bought Pontings, Barker was elected MP for Penyrn and Falmouth. He had a handsome house in Hertfordshire where he bred polo ponies and Syrian sheep, and in 1908 he was knighted.

Fortune seemed to be smiling broadly on the whole Barker Empire until the fateful night of 3 November 1912 when the new food hall block was the scene of a fatal fire. The fifth floor was still being used as dormitories for twenty people and five of these, all waitresses, were killed when they jumped prematurely from the windows. At the inquest, the firm's directors were criticised for not paying attention to the Fire Brigade's warnings about safety measures.

In the midst of the Christmas rush, the management, undeterred, took over vacant land on the Crown site opposite to erect temporary buildings which a decade or so later would be replaced by the Portland stone Ladymere building. The fire-gutted block was rebuilt in 1913-14 with a bridge linking it to the buildings in Ball Street and a subway running under the main road to the new departments on the north side.

John Barker retired in 1914 and died within months. That year the 34-year-old Trevor Bowen from Monmouthshire, who had been manager of Lyons Bakery near Olympia at Cadby Hall, was appointed manager of Barker's Food Section.

71. *In the John Barker Food Hall in June 1929.*

72. *A display of wedding cakes at John Barker's in the 1920s. They were being sold at 2/6d (12½p) per lb.*

73. Sir Sydney Skinner in 1922.

74. An early Derry and Toms shop at the corner of Wrights Lane, c.1875. Photo by Linley Sambourne.

THE WAR AND AFTER

In August 1914 Bowen was involved in the gigantic task of army catering – carried out by private contractors before the establishment of the Catering Corps. One of his first big contracts was the feeding of 'Kitchener's Army' waiting in depots to go overseas.

The chairmanship of Barker's was taken over by Sydney Skinner, the director who had been responsible for the Pontings take-over, known as 'Skinners folly'. Undeterred, (it is said that in his early career he had been sacked by his employer in Oxford Street for impertinence), it was Skinner who negotiated the merger with Derry and Toms in 1919.

He also inspired the formation of a Territorial Army unit amongst the employees, the 162 Anti-Aircraft Battery, which also served in the Second World War.

After the Armistice, Skinner, with Trevor Bowen now as co-director, looked ambtiously ahead. Among the more audacious of their plans was the closure of Ball Street to allow the store to be built out towards Kensington Square. Deals were made with the LCC and the Borough Council, who were united on the need for road widening of the High Street. Eventually, an agreement was reached in 1927 and Ball Street was closed while Skinner and Bowen visited America to study stores there. However, the private residents of Kensington Square were, according to *The Survey of London*, sorely tried by the 'Barkerization' of their amenities and increasingly well-organised. They resisted any further encroachment of their neighbourhood, but the battle was to continue for the next seventy years.

DERRY AND TOMS

The first building to be reconstructed was that of Derry and Toms. In 1924, a young architectural student, Bernard George, had joined the company, having worked as a student with the architect, Robert Atkinson, on earlier plans that included a roof garden Tea Room at Barker's. It was George, who during a long service, was to supervise the rebuilding not only of Derry's with its remarkable Roof Garden, but also Barker's. Work took three years to complete. Five floors included the magnificent Rainbow Room restaurant on the top floor. The exterior is described architecturally as Beaux-arts with an Egyptian theme; stone friezes are broken by bronze grilles depicting the signs of the zodiac.

The famous Roof Garden, with its terrace restaurant, was not completed until 1938 when the Earl of Athlone performed its official opening. It cost £25,000 and consisted of three areas, an English Garden, a Tudor Court and a Moorish garden with fountains, all divided by arches and follies. Its remarkable construction, on a bed of brick and rubble on a bitumen base allows for the shallowest possible soil, yet it supports full-grown trees as well as flower beds and shrubbery and a small stream ripples through it inhabited by water fowl, including flamingos. Ralph Hancock was responsible for its landscaping and planting. In its brief pre-war life it was 'opened' daily for charity by well-known personalities including royalty. During the war, when it had closed, a 250-pound bomb hit the garden but passed through to explode on the fourth floor. After the Barker Group was sold to the House of Fraser, the Roof Garden was leased for use as a restaurant and a night club.

REBUILDING BARKER'S

The rebuilding of the Barker store began in 1927 and was not completed until 1958, beset not only by the war but by restrictions and disputes afterwards. The extensions marooned Thackeray's House at 16 Young Street, which had been used by Barker's for its building department and there were fears that it might be demolished despite a vigorous campaign by the Kensington Society to save it. *The Kensington News* had it made plain to them by Barker's that their advertising revenue would be put seriously in jeopardy if they supported the campaign editorially just as they were also scolded for criticising the

practice of removing the Christmas decorations from the shop windows several days before the festival to allow sales goods to be displayed.

Sydney Skinner became seriously ill in 1940 and Trevor Bowen was appointed Chairman. The new building was also the work of Bernard George. The curved front has some carved stone work, showing items that might be bought within, and there are metallic decorations similar to Derry's. Post-war restrictions frustrated Bowen. He commenced a campaign for the widening of the road with banners on the old building saying 'Safety First – until Barker's widening scheme is completed this crossing is dangerous.' On 15 April 1955 the dream came true and the ceremonial hammer commencing the demolition was swung by Bowen himself with such enthusiasm that he narrowly missed hitting the mayor, Alderman Lady Petrie, on the head! When the foundation stone of his new building was laid a casket was placed with it containing coins, newspapers, including the *Kensington News*, and a film of the Roof Garden. In July 1957 the House of Fraser made a take-over bid for the Barker Group and the deal was completed in August, with Trevor Bowen, who liked to be known as 'Mr. Kensington' being made the Honorary President, a position he held until his death in 1965. He was given a handsome office in the Derry building, but he had little to do but recall past glories and reflect sadly on the fact that, despite the enormous role he had played in the commercial

75. Barker's ploy to hasten the rebuilding of their store, by urging the authorities to treat the narrow road as a safety hazard to the public.

76. The beginning of rebuilding the Barker's store in 1955. John Boyd-Carpenter, Minister of Transport, begins the work, with Trevor Bowen on the right.

history of Kensington for over fifty years, he was never offered a knighthood, blaming this on his clash with municipal leaders.

THE END OF AN EMPIRE

The House of Fraser first closed the Ladymere and Barker's store on the north side of the High Street, followed in 1970 by Pontings and Derry's which went to British Land and Dorothy Perkins in 1973. John Barker's has continued in token as one of the shops in the new Barker block, on the corner of Young Street, where all the upper floors are now the offices of the Northcliffe Group, publishers of the *Daily Mail*.

OTHER BIG NAMES

If there is a common thread that runs through the history of the Kensington High Street giants, Barker's, Derry and Toms and Pontings, it is that the men who made them were true shopkeepers as well as entrepreneurs. They are personified by one of the last of them, the Welshman, Trevor Bowen, who retained his provincial accent. He could be seen in the store every day, black jacket with a gold watch chain, striped trousers and a black Homburg hat, a 'floor-walker' of the kind that was then only associated with drapers in county towns, and this was in the 1960s

Of the big names, it was the Toms family who are first recorded in the High Street. A James Toms had a grocery shop on the south side of the main road in 1828 and is generally supposed to have been related to the Joseph Toms who ran a 'toy and fancy repository' in 1836, with his son, also Joseph. In the 1850s, the link with the Derry family was forged by the marriage of Joseph's elder sister, Christiana, to the young draper, Charles Derry, who had acquired a shop a few doors away on the corner of Wrights Lane. But it was with Christiana's younger brother, Charles Toms, with whom Derry set up the famous partnership in 1869. In 1871 the census showed the young Toms family: Charles was only 26, living above the partnership's new shops, nos. 107-111, with six female and eleven male assistants, two porters and three servants. In the following years more shops were acquired on either side, one of which, with a fourth storey added, accommodated a 'Moorish restaurant' reached by an open lift. Expansion westward was halted when a rival, the tailors, Tudor House Association, took two lots on which to build a double-fronted shop with flats above. This was a short-lived enterprise and by the turn of the century had been taken over by Derry and Toms who had their eyes on the premises behind the recently-vacated Tucker's candle factory. This enabled them to buy land behind houses in Kensington Square for packing and warehousing as well as taking leases of two houses there. These

77. *Crowds arriving at Kensington High Street station for a sale at Pontings in the 1950s.*

were used to accommodate some of the two-hundred live-in assistants in conditions which were vastly better than those usually associated with such hostels and included 'access to a fine library.'

The rebuilding of Kensington High Street station in 1912 and the closure of the Town Hall Tavern allowed Derry and Toms to join their old buildings to the new thus completing their dominance of this frontage, with a pretty turreted tower at the base of which was a ubiquitous Lyons Teashop and in the floors above, a small pet shop 'zoo'.

However this proved to be a swan song. The First World War affected all businesses but Derry and Toms, based on luxury goods and particularly famed for its millinery and gowns, suffered more than most. In 1920 the firm merged with Barker's while keeping its name and premises intact.

THE PONTING BROTHERS

The first of the Gloucestershire Ponting brothers to set up shop in London was Thomas, who in 1863 came to Archer Street, the western end of Westbourne Grove. William, Sydney and John joined him during the next few years. It was these younger men who moved to the High Street in 1873 to open what was first described as a 'small Berlin wool shop', a fashionable form of embroidery at that time. This grew into 'the largest fancy goods and silk business in London' on the site between High Street station and Wrights Lane. In 1893 they also acquired the now derelict Scarsdale House, using it first to board staff. In 1898 they became a limited company and continued to expand. The death of William Ponting, the largest shareholder, brought in non-family executives whose immediate action was to update the rather ramshackle but successful old shop into a handsome emporium. It was a costly enterprise and featured six storeys, two in the mansard roof, and a large basement. The stock included not only fashions, fabrics and millinery but also household goods, carpets, ironmongery, glass and china. Over a hundred of its assistants lived-in, enjoying amenities such as a billiard room. More buildings extended down the eastern side of Wrights Lane, and at the end of it all the firm was deeply in debt. Nevertheless, when the station was rebuilt to include a shopping arcade, Pontings took the whole of the space on their side, with an extension at the rear that included a galleried Fabric Hall under a glass roof. In 1906 their heavily mortgaged finances came to breaking point and they went into liquidation just before Christmas. Barker's acquired the whole business for £84,000 but continued to run it as an outwardly independent concern. After the First World War, when Barker's had also merged with Derry and Toms, Pontings was given a facelift

during which new display windows were installed and the big clock erected bearing the slogan 'Pontings – the House for Value.'

Scarsdale Terrace, at the far end of Wrights Lane, was used for a new mail order department and loading block to meet the demands of an ever-expanding mail order trade that continued through the Second World War and into the 1960s. Special trains were run to Kensington to bring the crowds to the sales at all three stores in the Barker Group and especially to Pontings Bargain Basement. At the entrance booth the much-advertised Mrs Naisby, with the patter of a market stall trader, but a more refined accent, could sell anything from stockings to household gadgets to a spellbound audience.

In 1970 Pontings was the first to be jettisoned by its parent company, by then the House of Fraser. For a while the premises, or at least part of them, became a bargain market until development was carried out to produce shops and offices, Pemberton House and Kensley House in Wrights Lane and William Cobbett House luxury flats.

BUYING UP

Seaman, Little and Co. on the site between Young Street and King (Derry) Street was the first to be swallowed up by their rivals, Barker's, in 1892. James Little, who ran the business is shown in the 1871 census as living over the shop with 19 shop assistants, four servants and three porters. The shop had opened ten years earlier and eventually employed a staff of 150 assistants in what they described as 'the finest show room in London' with mahogany counters and show cases. Barker's also attempted to buy up W. H. Hunt & Co., a general drapers established in 1889. This must have been to eliminate competition rather than for property expansion. This shop, at nos. 197-207, was on a site later occupied between the wars by Woolworth's. It says much for its popularity that it survived until 1923.

Another business which resisted the blandishments of Barker's was the redoubtable Pettit's, the drapers and outfitters opened by William Pettit in a shop on the corner of Allen Street and the High Street in 1886. This survived almost long enough to celebrate its centenary, but rising postal charges seriously affected its large mail order business. Changing fashions – Pettit's gloried in being old-fashioned, serving those who still needed woolly underwear and other comfortable but unglamorous garments – contributed to the firm's demise in 1977.

William Pettit opened his first shop only a few years before the rebuilding of what had been known as Bath Place by Henry Chesterton, by which time his humble premises had become a row of three shops. The basement and two floors represented

78. *Interior view of Seaman, Little & Co. The shop was founded in c.1861 and was bought up by Barker's in 1892.*

only a small proportion of space. The floors above them were occupied by a maze of corridors with rooms where the vast mail order business was carried out sending parcels all over the world from remote farms in Wales or Scotland to Australia, New Zealand, India and the Falkland Islands. But in William Pettit's day these floors were his home and living accommodation for many of his staff. A venerable figure with a white beard, he would drive up and down the High Street in a carriage with his talbot, a Dalmatian dog, running beside it.

When he retired he invited his chief shop walker, Thomas Hiscock, to take over the business. Thomas agreed and was eventually succeeded by his son, Ralph, and finally his grandson, Paul, whose reluctant decision it was to put the business into liquidation. The building is now a bookshop.

At the other end of the High Street, a fashionable dressmaker, Madame Kate Ker-Lane, appeared to be less considerate of her large staff of seamstresses than most of the more paternal shopkeepers with live-in staff. In 1905 she was summoned by factory inspectors for dangerous overcrowding with 43 dressmakers working on the four floors and basement of the narrow building with 'hardly any light on the stairs and in some places no hand rails'.

79. *Pettit's, drapers on the corner with Allen Street. Renowned for their woolly underwear.*

THE CANDLE FACTORY

One does not like to speculate on the conditions which might have existed at the old candle factory, a sprawling factory fronting the High Street. Tall chimneys belched smoke from the melting wax and long sheds housed the workers in what was a hazardous process.

The works had been founded in 1766 by James Wheble, a Hampshire man, who also owned a

80. The eastern end of Kensington High Street, opposite the entrance to the Palace. Madame Kate Ker-Lane's shop is to the far left. An enquiry found that she had a staff of 43 dressmakers working in dangerously overcrowded conditions there.

number of properties in Kensington including three houses in Kensington Square, in one of which, no. 36 he lived until his death in 1801, leaving a fortune of £200,000. A well-known Roman Catholic recusant, he was succeeded by another Catholic, John Kendall, one of the founders of the area's first Catholic chapel in Holland Street. When he died, in 1820, the business was bought by Francis Tucker, a candle maker from South Molton Street. The factory office and shop were on the High Street but the sprawling works behind filled the space between the railway lines and Burden Mews, demolished when Derry and Toms was rebuilt in 1927.

An entrance for carts was squeezed in beside the Duke of Abercorn, later the Town Hall Tavern. At this time the owner was Thomas Mosdell Smith, who was succeeded by his son, Henry Joseph, in 1873 when the firm had become the foremost supplier of candles to Roman Catholic churches all over the country. In 1900 a new factory was opened at Putney. From then on, however, business declined and in 1908 the company went into voluntary liquidation. The name and stock were taken up by Price's Patent Candle Company, which continued at Putney, Cricklewood and Battersea. The old Kensington site was sold to Derry and Toms and the Crown.

BIBA'S

Not all of Kensington's prominent businessmen had their names on shop fronts. Robert Jenkins, mayor

of the Royal Borough throughout the Second World War, had once sold eggs from a stall outside his father's grocery shop, Nicholls Stores, in Kensington Church Street. This shop became the interim home of Biba's between its early days in a converted chemist's shop in Abingdon Road, a sojourn in the vacated Daniel Neal's and its final glory in the Derry and Toms building.

The Biba story is legend. The designer Barbara Hulanicki and her husband Stephen FitzSimon rode on the 1960s fashion revolution. They began by selling fun clothes and very soon the little corner shop became too small. Using shopping trolleys or anything else on wheels they trundled the stock along the main road to Church Street where the old grocery, Nicholls Stores, was vacant. Biba's flourished there for some years until a deal was done and in 1973, in conjunction with British Land and Dorothy Perkins, Biba moved into the Art Deco Derry and Toms building. It had taken two years to become one of London's main tourist attractions. Sadly for its bold entrepreneurs, those who came more often looked and admired rather than bought, and in two years it had closed, to be replaced by the more down to earth Marks & Spencer and British Home Stores.

THE BIG CHEESE

A shopkeeper with influence in local affairs and on the development of Kensington was the cheesemonger, Jubal Webb. He was well-established on the south side of the High Street in the 1860s (his telegraphic address, 'Gorgonzola, London') but had to move to a site opposite, next to the parish church, during the 1869 Improvements. He was a long serving vestryman, a member of the Metropolitan Board of Works and a churchwarden. When the new bells were installed at St. Mary Abbots in 1879 he is photographed with fellow dignitaries and his name is inscribed on one of the bells. In 1893 he exhibited an enormous cheese weighing 22,000 pounds at the Chicago World Fair, its transportation presenting all sorts of difficulties. It was later returned to England and served at a banquet, by which time it must have been very ripe indeed!

When the London County Council was formed to succeed the Metropolitan Board of Works Webb had hopes of being elected but his opponents resurrected an old scandal from 1880, when he had been accused of using his position of High Constable to the Vestry to obtain money for licences. He was cleared, but it is rumoured that this was due to the skill of advocacy rather than his innocence.

In 1886 he had taken a house in The Terrace in the High Street and when this and the land behind it came up for sale he acquired it for £170,000. He first built the new Promenade of shops along the main

81. An advertisement for Biba's in 1974.

82. Jubal Webb (left in top hat) with his mammoth cheese.

road, then sold their freehold to the Crown in 1894 before continuing with his plans to develop the rest. These included the building of a concert or exhibition hall, which did not materialise.

He died in December 1901. Three years later his son was still flirting with the idea of building a theatre there, but once again it came to nothing.

THE ERARD FACTORY

In 1850 when the Crystal Palace was rising in Hyde Park, the French firm of piano and harp-makers, S. and P. Erard, built a factory in Kensington on a site to the east of Warwick Road. Established in Paris in 1780, they had a London branch in Great Marlborough Street and their reputation was high all over the world. The Kensington factory was built on much the same lines as their premises in Paris and consisted of two, long, dreary-looking four-storey buildings, with rows of small windows, a fragment of which was retained in the Barker's Depository which succeeded it. There were particular precautions against fire because of the stacks of timber, varnishes, polishes and other inflammable materials and many of the departments were sepa-

rated by thick iron doors. The owner, Pierre Erard, died in 1855 when the factory was producing a thousand instruments every year, but the business continued under the direction of his widow, the factory being enlarged in 1859 so that it covered four acres, and the staff was increased to over 300 people. But times were changing, Germany was offering cheaper mass-produced instruments and pianos were less popular in homes which were now often small flats or maisonettes. By 1881 the staff had decreased to 127. Madame Erard died in 1889 and the works closed the following year, all manufacturing being carried out in France, although the Great Marlborough Street showrooms were rebuilt to include a concert salon named for the founder.

PATRIOTIC PINTS

Despite its many public houses, old Kensington seems to have had only one brewery in the vicinity of the town centre. This was the Britannia, established in about 1834 by Edward Herington and William Wells. The new venture on a site in Allen Street now occupied by Allen Mansions, was ambitious; it was a purpose built industrial block with loading loft and arched entrance to the yard and stables. Sadly the enterprise did not pay. Known later as William Wells & Co. it was faced with bankruptcy in 1902 but recovered until 1924 when Young's bought it up. Only two of its outlets were left but these happily survive under their original names of the Britannia in Allen Street and the Britannia Tap in Warwick Road. The name came from the handsome statue that surmounted the building.

83. Kensington Toll Gate, c.1854, with the old cavalry barracks behind.

Turnpikes to Trains

In the early years of the eighteenth century hundreds of Turnpike Trusts were established by Acts of Parliament to manage roads with money collected at tollgates. The Kensington Turnpike trust was formed in 1726 to maintain the road from Hyde Park Corner to Addison Bridge. The main Kensington Toll Gate stood approximately at the present junction of Kensington Road and Palace Gate, and there was another at the southern end of Church Street.

The Trusts were notorious for their crooked dealings and were frequently attacked in broadsheets and newspapers. The tollgates were situated at junctions almost impossible to avoid. The traders complained that they discouraged potential customers, and the customers complained that the toll added to the price of everything they bought. Henry Fox went so far as to reposition the main entrance to Holland House just east of the tollgate so that he would not be inconvenienced during his journeys to town. There was general rejoicing when many of the London tollgates were abolished in 1864.

THE RAILWAYS ARRIVE

The Metropolitan and District Railway transformed Kensington High Street from a homely shopping street into a fashionable parade patronised by those who would normally go to the West End of London. But it was kept well out of sight. Once the disruption of its cut-and-cover construction was over, the scars were covered, and the trains could hardly be seen except in the stations. They ran behind the backs of houses or beneath them, in short tunnels and only came out into the open at basement level between the high cliffs of sooty grey bricks to let off steam before disappearing again. There were complaints, of course, from those who said they shook the houses and killed the garden shrubs with their sulphurous fumes.

In 1864 the Metropolitan Railway, having successfully opened its first line from Farringdon Road to Paddington, applied to extend it further to South Kensington via Notting Hill and Kensington High Street. This was agreed as part of a general plan to build what became the Circle Line, with the Metropolitan responsible for its construction on its northern arc from South Kensington to the Tower of London and the District Railway from South Kensington to Mansion House with the remaining gap as a joint construction. At the

84. Railway and sidings at Warwick Road in the 1930s.

same time the District Railway was given leave to build two short spurs from South Kensington to West Brompton and to Addison Road to meet the new West London railway.

The positioning of lines and stations was contentious since the advantages of having such local transport and the nuisance caused to properties had to be balanced. The complexity of the route and problems of land acquisition often produced awkward areas where the lines converged, such as the famous Cromwell Curve, a large triangle of land between Cromwell Road, Lexham Gardens and Emperors Gate, and that at Warwick Road, Earls Court. The latter was utilised for the Earls Court Exhibition and the Cromwell Curve was rafted over to build the West London Air Terminal.

Construction in the mid nineteenth century demanded considerable engineering skills. At the Cromwell Curve the Metropolitan engineer, John Fowler, constructed a 12-foot wide, 75 foot long bridge, said to be the first concrete arch bridge in the world, which remained in place for less than five years until the Metropolitan line was completed and opened on 1 October 1868.

The first Kensington station (High Street was added later to the name), was a single storey building with a small booking hall from which stairs descended to the platforms. The whole was covered by a massive iron-frame and glass roof. This arrangement was demolished in 1906 when a new station with a shopping arcade was built, the platforms then being covered only by canopies. The arcade and booking hall were renovated in 1937 at a time when huge crowds used the

station to go to the Summer and Winter sales at the High Street department stores.

MR PUNCH'S RAILWAY

At the western end of the High Street, within yards of the Hammersmith boundary, another railway was struggling to compete. It had begun as a replacement for a canal (*see* pp. 38-40), and at first was named prosaically the Birmingham, Bristol & Thames Junction Railway. It opened in 1844, connecting the Great Western junction at Willesden to the canal basin just south of Addison Road. It went, so it was said, 'from nowhere to nowhere' and it was hardly surprising that it was scarcely used by passengers.

So badly did it prosper in this respect that it was lampooned as 'Mr Punch's Railway', from its frequent appearances in that journal. It closed to passenger traffic in November 1844, only six months after its opening. The line continued to be used for freight, especially coal, but in 1863 its potential was increased when an extension was built along the old canal bed to connect the line over a new Thames bridge at Chelsea to Clapham Junction.

Taken over by the London North Western and the Great Western, the tracks were used by a number of other companies including the Hammersmith & City, a line that became part of the Metropolitan. In an attempt to attract passengers again all sorts of routes were devised to take workers to a variety of stations by ingenious systems of splitting trains in two at various points.

85. Addison Road station earlier this century, with Olympia on the left and an array of railway tracks for both steam and District Line trains. This successor to 'Mr Punch's Railway' marks the boundary of Kensington and Hammersmith.

The growth of its many rivals once again threatened its existence and soon its use was confined mainly to visitors to events at Olympia.

In 1940 passenger use ceased again, although the large sidings at what was known as Addison Road station served as marshalling yards for wartime supplies including munitions, and it became a target for enemy aircraft. The series of junctions to which the yards were connected made it also useful for troop movements and after the evacuation of Dunkirk many of the returning troops were first seen from trains passing through on their way to the midlands or the north. In present times private sector investment is attempting to utilise its facilities in new lines and a large housing development is taking place on surplus railway land along the west side of Russell Road.

THE FAST ROAD

In 1869, the *Kensington News* reported that 'a fast four-horse coach now passes though Knightsbridge and Kensington en route for Windsor. It is placed on the road by the Four in Hand Club and Lord Carrington drove on the inaugural journey on Tuesday.'

Even after the arrival of the railway, horse-drawn road transport was still the main way to get from here to there. Thackeray delighted in the frequent horse bus service within yards of his house in Young Street in 1846, and in her memoirs, his daughter, Anne Ritchie, recalled journeys made with her father on omnibuses or by hired cab. On one occasion, on their way to visit Edwin Landseer at St John's Wood, Thackeray decided on the spur of the moment to buy the fly and horse and employ 'the old white coachman', dressing him in a fine new uniform with 'Thackeray buttons'. The novelist thus became a member of the carriage class.

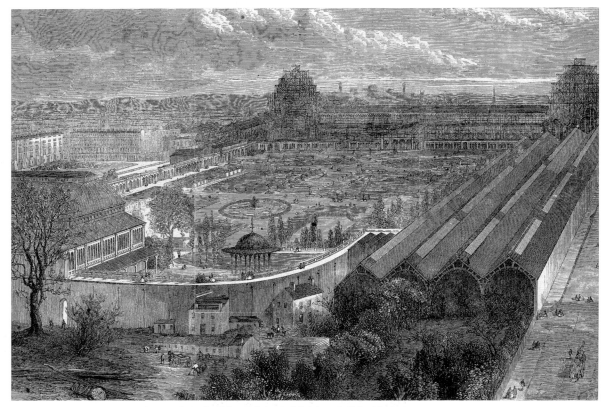

86. The Horticultural Garden, and the building of the Exhibition Hall in 1862.

A Cultural Suburb

EXHIBITIONISM

When the Crystal Palace was opened in Hyde Park in 1851, on a site between Alexandra Gate and the Knightsbridge barracks, much of the surrounding area consisted of market and horticultural gardens with a scattering of country estates. The Exhibition, encouraged zealously by Prince Albert and ably administered by Henry Cole, was a resounding success. So much so there were funds left over from the receipts to go on to a more permanent project, no less than a cultural centre on 87 acres between what is now Cromwell Road and Kensington Road. To this end, the Commissioners for the Exhibition, a body which continued to function after the Crystal Palace was dismantled, bought the 21 acres of the Gore Estate and the much larger Villars-Harrington Estate.

The project revolved around the flair and energies of three men – Prince Albert, who died in 1861

before much had been accomplished, Henry Cole the civil servant, and a young captain in the Royal Engineers, Francis Fowke who stretched his architectural and engineering talents to the limit. It was he that made the original design for the Albert Hall and on his death it was completed by a colonel in the same regiment.

THE SHOW GARDEN

Another attraction at what was called South Kensington, was the Royal Horticultural Society Garden. This also enjoyed the patronage of Prince Albert. Fowke designed a building in cast iron 265 x 96 x 75 feet high, that had gas lighting and a great staircase leading to a terrace walk. He also included a number of water features based on artesian wells.

The Garden was opened by the Prince in June 1861. He spoke of uniting the science and art of gardening with the skills of sculpture, painting and architecture. He envisaged the Garden being a very popular attraction, but the Society had more

87. Fashionable crowds enjoying the attractions of the 1862 Exhibition.

exclusive ideas and did little to encourage the general public. Indeed they feared that the 1862 Exhibition being planned next door would threaten their privacy and they might be 'subjected to disagreeable annoyance and comment from the windows of the refreshment room'.

The site, so near London, was not ideal, for smoke pollution had an adverse effect on cultivation. In 1876 the Society surrendered its lease to the Commissioners who had plans to build a Science Museum on much of the site.

1862 AND ALL THAT

The Exhibition building for 1862 covered 23 acres. Designed by Fowke, it had none of the elegance of the Crystal Palace, and it was derided in the *Building News* as one of the ugliest buildings ever raised in this country. Enormous brick walls rose straight from the pavements of Cromwell and Exhibition Roads and Queens Gate, with two great domes at either end. The Prince was less enthusiastic about this project and, in any case, died before it was opened.

The Exhibition was less nationalistic than the 1851 event, but it continued the tradition of showing how art and manufacture can be intertwined.

Separate sections featured machinery in motion, carriages and cabs, groups of statuary, displays of jewellery including the Kohinoor diamond, gold and silver plate and an impressive array of armaments.

Financially, the Exhibition was not a success, receipts falling £10,000 short of expenditure. After that, how to dispose of the great pile? It was taken down and sold for scrap, some of it being used to build another white elephant, the Alexandra Palace in north London.

MUSEUMLAND

The dream was to make the area a cultural centre and to bring useful education to the public masses. In 1855 Parliament made a grant of £55,000 to construct a temporary museum in which to house a design collection then at Marlborough House. The site chosen for this building, then called the South Kensington Museum, on the south-east corner of Exhibition Road, included the former home of the nurseryman, Henry Wise (*see* p.117).

Prince Albert himself had sketched a rough idea of how he thought the building should look but its eventual construction was overseen by the engineer Sir William Cubitt together with a firm that specialised in exporting corrugated iron buildings to the colonies. It was thus a very utilitarian building constructed mainly of corrugated iron. The exterior was painted with green and white stripes, to resemble a tent, and a screen of shrubbery was planted.

The Marlborough House collections were joined by a hotchpotch of others from the Architectural Museum, the Museum of Construction and the Economic Museum which was devoted to household management and food.

The opening ceremony was performed by Queen Victoria on 24 June 1857 and although the Museum was considered to be desirable it was criticised for its looks and its location. Initially a site for a railway station was earmarked but a government committee felt that the lack of such transport had not stopped enormous numbers of working-class visitors to the Great Exhibition, and therefore did not encourage the scheme. It was not until 1868 that South Kensington station was opened.

To allow working-class people to visit it, the Museum was open on two evenings a week. 'The poor need no longer mourn that the ample page of knowledge, rich with the spoils of time, is a sealed book to the lowly', and during the first month of its opening there were 14,000 visitors.

88. The 'Brompton Boilers', the first South Kensington Museum. The Brompton Oratory is to the right. This photograph was taken by Rupert Potter, father of Beatrix Potter, on 11 July 1899.

THE VICTORIA AND ALBERT

The Kensington Museum soon ran out of room and untidy extensions appeared. In 1890 the architect Aston Webb won the competition to build a new Museum which Queen Victoria, who laid the foundation stone in 1899, asked should be called the Victoria & Albert Museum. Edward VII opened the completed building in June 1909 and, rather belatedly in tribute, a Cole Wing was added in 1983. A controversial addition, designed by Daniel Libeskind, to sit beside the main building has recently been proposed.

Today, the V & A is the country's major museum of applied arts and extends its influence with loan exhibitions. Its staff are also in charge of the collections at Ham House, Apsley House and Osterley.

'GODLESS' SCIENCE

Prince Albert thought science to be rather 'godless', though he wished to encourage it especially its use in manufacturing industries. The early South Kensington Museum had some scientific exhibits but their scope and display provoked Professor T.H. Huxley to urge that a Science Museum should be set up and 'removed from its

89. The new Victoria & Albert Museum. Drawing by Frank L. Emanuel, 1907.

present filthy repulsive, unwholesome sheds' there. But it was not until the summer of 1914 that the building of a Science Museum began and then it was used as government offices during the war. It was only in March 1928 that one block was opened as a Science Museum by George V. Further work was delayed by the Second World War, but it was completed in 1961.

ELEPHANTS AND WHALES

In July 1858, a group of eminent naturalists, led by Sir Richard Owen, urged Disraeli, then Chancellor of the Exchequer, to rehouse the collection of zoological, geological, botanical and mineralogical items then at the British Museum, in a separate building – a Natural History Museum. Any tendency on the part of Owen towards Darwinism was dispelled by his intention to include 'examples of the power of the Creator', such as the largest specimens of elephants and whales.

In 1864 the ubiquitous Fowke won the competition to design this new museum. However, within a year he was dead and the 36-year-old Alfred Waterhouse was invited to take over the implementation of Fowke's plan. But with governmental changes and delays, building did not begin until 1873 and it was to be another eight years before it was opened to the public. Fortunately, Waterhouse was allowed to design his own building rather than modify Fowke's plan, and he produced one of the most notable of London buildings. Extensions since then have included an entomological block (1949-52), a northern block (1959), a Botanical Gallery (1963) and a new wing on the corner of Exhibition Road by James Ellis and John Pinckheard (1977).

A GEM OF A PLACE

The youngest and smallest of the institutions, the Geological Museum, was squeezed unwillingly at first between the Natural History and the Science Museums. Its roots go back to 1835 when Henry Thomas de la Beche, the first Director of Geological Survey, urged that a museum should be established to display samples of rocks and minerals which had a bearing on industry. In May 1851 a Museum of Practical Geology was opened by Prince Albert at 28 Jermyn Street but it did not move from this valuable site until after the First World War, during which it had been damaged by bombing. The new building at South Kensington was completed in 1933, but emphasis was placed on study and research rather than 'the delectation of the general public' and, to a layman, it was rather dull.

In the post-war years it has made a determined attempt to attract visitors. The two extremes of new pre-historic finds and space exploration have now been used to display an arresting 'Story of the Earth'.

EMPIRE BUILDING

To the rear of the Victoria & Albert Museum still stands the 287-foot tower which is all that remains of the old Imperial Institute – the tower is now part of the Imperial College campus.

The Institute began as an Indian section in the South Kensington Museum but the Prince of Wales, later Edward VII, saw it as a basis for an Empire Museum as part of the celebrations for his mother's approaching Jubilee. An appeal brought in donations from all over the empire. The building was designed by T.E. Colcutt and Queen Victoria laid the foundation stone – granite from the Cape, on a pedestal of Indian bricks – in July 1887. It included two flanking towers both 176 feet high at each end of the 750-foot frontage. The copper dome of the central tower, now turquoise with age, included a bell chamber of 200 feet containing the Alexandra Ring of ten bells, each named for a member of the royal family, a gift of an Australian woman.

However, the Institute ran into severe financial difficulties and was not rescued until 1898 when the government discharged its debts, but at the same time allocating half the building to the University of London.

For the first half of this century the Institute became increasingly involved in education. In 1953 plans were already afoot for the expansion of Imperial College but it was not until three years later that the public learnt that these would involve the demolition of the Institute.

After a prolonged campaign of protest the Queen's Tower, as it is known, was retained as a compromise and the chimes still ring out on State occasions. When demolition began in 1957 plans had already been announced for the new Commonwealth Institute in 3½ acres of Holland Park. The design of this, with its tent-like copper roof (the copper donated by the Chamber of Mines of the former Northern Rhodesia), was the work of the architects Sir Robert Matthew and Johnson-Marshall. Commonwealth countries gave other materials, especially various woods. The interior, with its sweeping central staircase and open-plan galleries, was the work of James Gardner.

In present times the Institute's future has still appeared insecure despite its active role in education which attracts thousands of school visits every year, and a variety of specialist exhibitions.

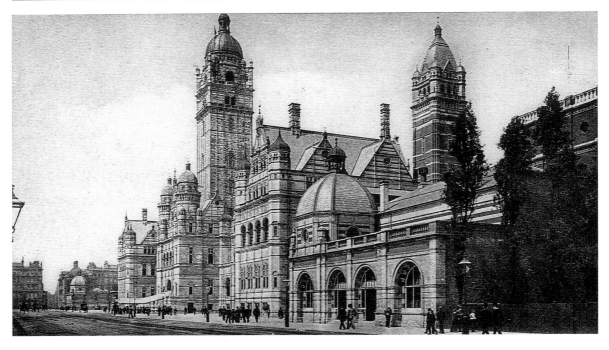

90. The Imperial Institute, c.1905.

NEW COLLEGES

The gradual development of Museumland was complemented by the foundation of various colleges in the vicinity.

In 1881 the Normal School of Science and the Royal School of Mines were housed in a new building in Exhibition Road. Departments there included mathematics, astronomy, botany, agriculture, mineralogy, metallurgy and geology. Renamed the Royal College of Science in 1890, the building continued to serve various departments into the 1980s.

The Royal College of Art originated in the Metropolitan College of Design, established in 1837 in Somerset House. It moved to the South Kensington Museum in 1863, where it occupied a building in Exhibition Road. Here it remained in inadequate accommodation until 1961 when a new eight-storey building was opened in Kensington Gore.

Queen Victoria's third daughter, Princess Christian, founded what became the Royal School of Needlework in Sloane Street in 1872 to revive the art of embroidery. All those involved were 'gentlewomen by birth' – even those employed in the showrooms. By 1892 it had been granted a site on the corner of Imperial Institute and Exhibition Roads, where a handsome building was erected to the design of Fairfax Wade. When the building was leased to Imperial College, the school moved first to Princes Gate in 1949, and in the 1980s to Hampton Court. The grand old buliding was demolished in 1962.

As for music, it was thought that a training school with a wider acceptance of students than the elite of the Academy of Music at Marylebone was desirable. The entrepreneur builder, Charles Freake, built the Royal College of Music at his own cost and the Commissioners leased him a site to the west of the later Albert Hall. Here 'the strange sounds of practising would be least inconvenient to the neighbourhood'. Henry Cole's architect son, Lt. H. Cole of the Royal Engineers, gave his services free. The frontage of the building was decorated with sgriaffito work designed by the teacher at the National Art Training School, F.W. Moody, and executed by his students. The building was completed in 1875 and opened with Sir Arthur Sullivan as Principal in 1876. When the College needed a larger site only a few years later the building was handed over to the Royal College of Organists, which had been founded in 1863.

A new music college was built on the south side of Prince Consort Road and the foundation stone was laid in July 1890, when the brass band of Samson Fox's Leeds Forge 'nearly blew the mar-

91. (Top) *The Royal School of Needlework.*

92. (Below) *The Royal College of Music.*

quee away'. Ironmaster Samson Fox had given £30,000 towards the cost of the building. The College, built to the design of Arthur Blomfield, had separate entrances and staircases for men and women students.

Expansion, with additions to the various schools and colleges continued through the periods both before and after the First and Second World Wars as the departments were extended to keep pace with scientific progress. In 1951 foundations were actually laid for the new chemical technology and aeronautical building but were held up by a shortage of steel. This proved a blessing in disguise, as two years later the government decided that if university level was to be maintained, Imperial College, as it was named in 1909, must be extended to accommodate nearly 5,000 students.

When details of a vast rebuilding plan were made public in 1956 they may have pleased the academic hierarchy but were greeted by the general public with vehement opposition on several grounds.

In its annual report for 1955-56, the College reassured critics that although the buildings would be large and functional, 'they would not be modern in the vulgar sense or clash with the pleasant legacies of the past'.

The architects were Norman and Dawbarn. Building went on throughout the sixties and well into the seventies and in addition to the erection of the departments, College Block, Great Hall, Archives and Library, student accommodation was provided in Princes Square. Here, to designs by Richard Sheppard and Partners, Weeks Hall was built together with a sports centre. The new buildings were served by several new roads – Wells Way, Callan, Arms and Frankland Roads, the latter named for Sir Edward Frankland, the Victorian laboratory designer.

93. The Royal College of Organists.

94. The brickwork undercroft of the Albert Memorial.

ALBERT'S MEMORIALS

Prince Albert deserves a memorial in 'South Kensington', and he has two. One is the massive monument opposite the Royal Albert Hall, recently restored to its full magnificence.

It was designed by Sir George Gilbert Scott, who was made 'positively ill' by the dramas associated with its construction. Scott said later that he had given the memorial the character of a great shrine, 'surrounded by sculpture illustrating the arts and sciences that he [Albert] fostered and the great undertakings which he originated'.

At the time the memorial was in its early planning stages it was competing for government money with the great concert hall it was to face. Fortunately, the builder of the memorial, John Kelk, agreed to do the work at cost price and pay for any excess over the estimate. It did, in fact, cost about £1,000 less and Kelk installed the flight of granite steps leading up to the Memorial free of charge.

The Memorial stands on a honeycomb of brick arches on a concrete base 17 feet thick. The Irish and Scotch granite was worked on the site, the cutting, by axe, and the polishing (all by hand) being carried out by a team of masons working day and night in relays. During the severe winter of 1866-67 fires had to be lit to prevent the water used in the process from freezing.

The Queen herself chose the sculptor for the Prince's statue, Baron Carlo Marochetti, who lived at Onslow Square. Proposals to have either an equestrian or standing figure were turned down and Marochetti was still working on alternatives when he died. Henry Foley was chosen as his successor and eventually, after much disagreement, it was decided that the figure should be sitting down looking at the Great Exhibition catalogue. More misfortune occurred. Foley became ill while working on the figure in the open and this led to his death only months before the figure was to be cast, and then another delay occurred because of the death of the owner of the casting factory. Famous sculptors were contracted to do the other figures surrounding that of Albert and the bas relief frieze around the podium.

The Memorial, minus the statue of Albert, was opened to the public in 1872, and the long-awaited central figure was put in place in 1876.

95. Construction of the Albert Memorial.

96. 'Asia', one of the groups surrounding the Albert Memorial.

THE UNWANTED STATUE

Another statue of Albert stands west of the Royal Albert Hall, though at first it was located in the Horticultural Society's Garden. It was first mooted after the success of the Great Exhibition, but Albert declined. 'I would much rather not be made the prominent feature of such a monument, as it would both disturb my quiet rides in Rotten Row to see my own face staring at me, and if (as is very likely) it became an artistic monstrosity, like most of our monuments, it would upset my equanimity...'

Despite his reservations the project went ahead but later the figure of Britannia was substituted. She was then superseded by a statue of the Queen, but before it was completed Albert died and instead he was made the subject again. The memorial was unveiled on 10 June 1863.

97. The Albert Memorial. Prince Albert is looking at a catalogue for the Great Exhibition of 1851.

98. Construction of the Royal Albert Hall.

THE STATELY MUSIC DOME

It had been the intention of Prince Albert and Henry Cole to include a concert/conference hall at South Kensington. In 1857 Cole produced a plan for a huge amphitheatre in which '30,000 people could be assembled and practise chorus singing' instead of succumbing to more 'debasing pursuits and temptations'.

The cost of this was too much and ten years later Cole was still making plans, albeit for a much smaller building. Once again, Francis Fowke was the architect, but he was still working on his designs when he died in 1865. Henry Scott of the Royal Engineers was brought in to take over the project, and it was under his direction that the hall became an ellipse rather than a circle.

The construction of the dome was regarded by *The Builder* as a great engineering triumph, but the acoustics were unsatisfactory for most of its life; in 1968-69 fibreglass diffusers were fitted which substantially cured the problem.

The opening ceremony was held on 29 March 1871 and attended by the Queen, making one of her very rare public appearances since the death of the Prince. No public funds were expended on the project, but on the other hand most of the best seats were sold in perpetuity to subscribers and therefore left the Hall short of income for the forseeable future.

99. *Calisthenic and marching exercises before the Prince and Princess of Wales at the Royal Albert Hall in 1888.*

100. *The Royal Albert Hall as portrayed in its early days by the Illustrated London News.*

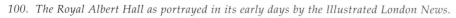

Rich Men at the Gate

THE BUILDING OF HYDE PARK GATE

Sir Baptist Hicks, the first Viscount Campden, and his wife may have been very rich but from the lofty height of their home on Campden Hill they did not entirely forget the poor. On their respective deaths, in 1629 and 1643, bequests were made by each to the benefit of the poor of the parish. Lady Campden specified that the sum of £200 should be used to purchase land in Kensington yielding an income of at least £10 a year, half of which should be used 'for the better relief of the most poor and needy people of good life and conversation' and the other half to put 'a poor boy to apprenticeship'. The Campden Charities have grown vastly over the centuries.

Their Trustees bought six acres of land known as Butts Field, on the corner of Kensington Road and Hogmire Lane (now Palace Gate/Gloucester Road) and let it to a local man on a 25-year lease at £10 a year. After a century or so some of the charities' money was used to build a workhouse. No pictures survive of this first institution but the historian, Thomas Faulkner, describes it in 1820 as a 'substantial brick building'. In 1828, five houses, part of today's Hyde Park Gate, were built on the main road, all later replaced by blocks of flats, including Broadwalk House. It was not until the mid-1830s that these were accompanied by the 'frying pan' layout of Hyde Park Gate, with a central garden and two grand houses, Cleeve Lodge and Stoke Lodge, nos. 42 and 45, built at the far end of the cul-de-sac, the latter being the home of the Italian opera singer, Guilia Grisi, in 1851.

In 1833 a piece of waste land to the east of Butts Field, described as the haunt of one or two donkeys, was bought by schoolmaster, Joshua Flesher Hanson, who seems to have found property speculation more

101. Nos. 1 and 1a Hyde Park Gate.

rewarding than teaching. He was at that time engaged in developments in the nearby Kensington New Town and Campden Hill Square. The donkeys went and mansions soon began to rise in another cul-de-sac which Hanson also called Hyde Park Gate, a name used also for the whole terrace of houses on the main Kensington Road between Queens Gate and de Vere Gardens.

Hanson's houses had Corinthian columns, Ionic porches and Doric pillars and were very grand indeed, as were their occupants, dukes and duchesses, statesmen, merchants, lawyers and landowners. More famously, Vanessa (Bell) and Virginia (Woolf) daughters of Sir Leslie Stephen, the first editor of *The Dictionary of National Biography*, were born at no. 22 and spent their childhood years there, as did Robert Baden Powell at no. 9. More recently, Winston Churchill, attracted by its privacy, made his home at 27-28 Hyde Park Gate from 1945 until his death in 1965, apart from his years as Prime Minister at 10 Downing Street.

The cul-de-sac developments screened the early residents from the sight and sound of the neighbouring workhouse on the other part of Butts Field, but in 1843, with the building of a new workhouse in Marloes Road, the Campden Charities soon sold the site of the old building to John Inderwick, the tobacco importer whose successors until recently had a business in the West End, and who was already engaged in developments in Kensington New Town. Inderwick demolished the old workhouse

and began work on what was to become Kensington Gate. Leigh Hunt was not impressed by the style of architecture, saying that the house on the corner of Gloucester Road, with a round tower, looked like a 'pepper box' or a 'trifle from Margate'. Nevertheless the houses sold and by 1861 their occupants included more 'ladies of title', merchants, lawyers, a mine-owner and the sculptor, Richard Westmacott, whose household consisted of eleven people of whom five were servants.

PALACE GATE

In 1804, when the northern end of Hogmire Lane was still little more than a cart track, George Aust, Secretary of the Royal Hospital at Chelsea, had a house built on its north west corner at the junction with Kensington Road. Called Noel House, and set back from the main highway, it was surrounded by a large garden designed by his wife, who, as the Hon. Mrs Murray, wrote a guidebook *The Beauties of Scotland*. Noel House didn't last long – it was demolished in 1861 after purchase by the Cubitt building firm.

Cubitts soon persuaded their neighbouring landowners, the Campden Charities, that 'a great public benefit' would result if one fine street were created between their two properties by moving the line of Hogmire Lane to the west. The Charities' Trustees agreed and Palace Gate was laid out and once again the great houses began to go up. Among the first,

102. *'Noel House, Kensington Gore, the Residence of G. Aust Esqr.', c.1808.*

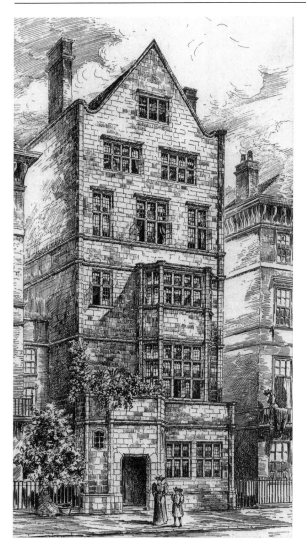

103. No. 1a Palace Gate, once the home of John Forster.

104. John Everett Millais.

1a was taken by historian and biographer, John Forster, who wrote his life of Dickens there and also used it to house his famous library. After Forster's death the house was taken by James Johnstone, a member of the family which owned the *Standard* newspaper, who employed a host of famous names in the Arts and Crafts movement on its lavish décor. When it was completed *The Studio* described it as 'having distinction written all over it, a house of today built for a gentleman by a gentleman.'

At the other end of Palace Gate, on the corner of Canning Place, another house was built for Reginald Cholmondeley, a wealthy landowner and a talented

sculptor. At no. 2 the owner was John Everett Millais, who had bought the site for £8,400 in 1876 and moved in from his home at 7 Cromwell Place in 1876. Described as 'a great, plain, square house, with only an excrescence here and there', it showed no sign of the influence that the fashionable aesthetic movement was having on the homes of others. Not long after, Oscar Wilde would set up his fanciful house in Tite Street but Millais had 'not so much as a peacock fan' in sight. It was instead a 'beautiful house of a household.' Even the studio, a wing at the back, although having the appearance of a comfortable sitting room, had practical lighting and storage and facilities for the easy movement of large canvases. Nevertheless, there were elegant and expensive refinements, such as the indoor fountain by the sculptor J. Edgar Boehm. Millais lived there until his death in 1896.

On the eastern corner of Palace Gate the Duke of Bedford bought two plots in 1879 with the intention of building what was almost a palace, although he already had a very elegant home in Belgrave Square. It is speculated that the nobleman wished to be nearer his mistress, who was living in Leonard Place, but the lady died before the house was completed and the Duke never lived there. Its first occupant was James Watney, the MP for East Surrey.

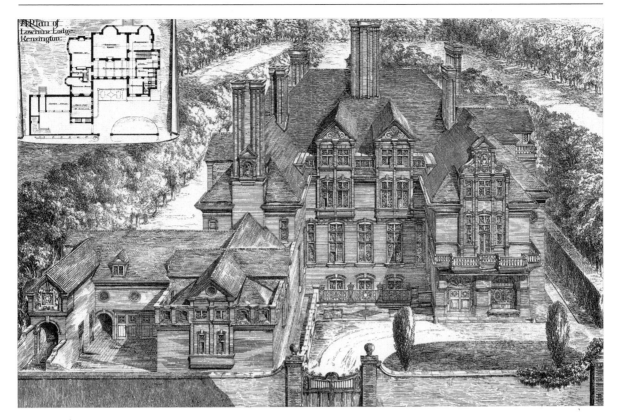

105. *Lowther Lodge, c.1872.*

Built regardless of cost, its layout included a 50-foot long drawing room and library, a WC on each floor and hot and cold water supply. Nineteen 'register stoves' provided heating and gas was laid on throughout the house. Once again its life was short, barely thirty years, being sold in 1898 when it was planned to build flats on the site, a scheme successfully resisted for a while by other residents of Palace Gate but achieved in 1905 to build Thorney Court. This in turn was replaced by a block of service apartments in 1972, its demolition being condemned by the Kensington Society as 'most unwarranted.'

It is not often that a block of flats is more interesting than the large house it preceded. But this is the case with no. 10 Palace Gate where 'Bleasedale' was demolished in 1937 to build the most unusual maisonettes in London. Planned on a system known as 'three/two' to the designs of the Anglo-Canadian architect, Wells Coates, two floors on one side of the block equal three on the other, providing rooms of different heights as well as flexibility in the allocation of accommodation.

THE PRIVATE BUILDERS

The Commissioners of the 1851 Exhibition were beset with money troubles as their ambitious plans went ahead. An obvious source of revenue was the leasing of some of their outlying land for building developments and among the first of these was a group of handsome buildings on the west side of Queens Gate (nos. 9-19), designed by Charles Richardson.

The cleverest of all the speculating builders was Charles James Freake (1814-1884). From inauspicious beginnings – his father was a coal merchant who later became a publican of the Royal Oak in Pimlico – he was said at his death to have 'made the neighbourhood of South Kensington, raising it from a neglected suburb to the rank of a second Belgravia.' Knighted in 1882, he never lost his cockney accent and it is an indication of the strength of his personality that it was not long before he had persuaded his genteel wife to adopt his vowel sounds and dropped 'h's.

Having described himself as a builder in earlier days he changed this later to 'architect/builder'. By 1860 he was living in one of his own grand houses, no. 21 Cromwell Road, opposite the site of the proposed 1862 Exhibition with his wife and daughter and three female relations, a butler, footman and seven other servants. The rear of the house had a ballroom that could also be used for theatrical performances and concerts, for he was very fond of entertaining his guests, who often included the Prince of Wales.

Freake had previously worked around Onslow Square and at the time of the Commissioners' first moves to acquire land he was already planning to develop the stretch along Kensington Road. The three-pronged Princes Gate Mews, together with sites on the frontage of Exhibition Road, were part of a swap he carried out with the Commissioners who needed access to the main highway through his land at this point.

Another builder involved in developments on the perimeter of the Commissioners' land was William Douglas, a house agent and upholsterer, who had come to London from Scotland in 1837. But his developments fell victim to fashion. The rich wanted Norman Shaw's 'Queen Anne' revival rather than Douglas's Italianate and his empty houses were often converted into flats or even refaced to satisfy the new fashion. In 1888 Douglas was declared bankrupt and died in 1893 but his son, John, took over the business. He became a Kensington councillor and it was his son, Quentin, who was mayor 1952-53.

The Commissioners were frustrated in their efforts to buy Eden Lodge, a rambling house with an extensive garden on the north-west corner of Exhibition Road, named by George Eden, a Governor General of India. Even in 1870, when the house was eventually sold, the Commissioners failed to buy it and it went instead to William Lowther, MP who commissioned Shaw to design a house for him, demolishing the old lodge. The new house, Lowther Lodge, was described as 'half way between a town and country home'. Lowther remained here until his death in 1912, when his son, James Lowther, speaker of the House of Commons, sold it to the Royal Geographical Society. In 1927 the Society granted a lease for the block of flats, Princes Gate Court, to be built in the garden.

Shaw's style of architecture was enjoying a wave of popularity as Lowther Lodge neared completion. In 1874 a rich young stockbroker, J.P. Heseltine, who was also a talented etcher and art connoisseur, engaged him to design no. 196 Queens Gate. The *Building News* declared that 'were there more such houses, London would be vastly less monotonous and more worthy of being the British metropolis and chief city in the world'. Heseltine, who gave a lavish children's fancy dress party as a housewarming, remained in the house until 1925. It has now been converted into flats, but survives.

Norman Shaw houses which did not survive include no. 180 Queens Gate which he built for barrister H. F. Makins, an art connoisseur and collector. The Makins family retained the house until it made way for the Imperial College redevelopment in 1971. Wartime bombing was to blame for the destruction of no. 185 Queens Gate which Norman Shaw designed for stockbroker, William Vivian; this featured a huge two story inner hall. This house eventually passed to the Maison d'Institute de France. A friend of Heseltine, a City cement manufacturer, Frederick Anthony White, was so taken with his friend's house that he too came to live in Queens Gate at no. 170, where the house Shaw made for him remains as part of the new Imperial College.

FIRST FLATS

In 1875 the Commissioners were looking for buyers for the land to the east of the Albert Hall, an awkwardly shaped area owing to the curved road on the southern side. First plans proposed six or seven large houses, or a suite of club chambers. The final choice rested on a design by Norman Shaw whom the Commissioners were so keen to use that they offered to employ him at their own expense. The five storeys of Albert Hall Mansions, huge flats with the amenities of large houses such as pantries, closets and dressing rooms, began to rise facing the Park. The three blocks were completed in 1887 and the following year it was decided to let two sites on either side of the newly-established Prince Consort Road (only the north side materialised). A modern estate agent has described the resultant Albert Court as 'turreted splendour…. its entrance hall alone is a shade short of a hundred yards in length with fire places, long case clocks, minstrels' galleries, even a post box … less of a corridor and more of a roadway … designed to allow horse drawn carriages to drive right through the middle of the block to set down their passengers without fear of getting wet if the weather was bad.'

This is a charming supposition but it is more likely that its form was the result of an awful financial situation which left it partially unbuilt for over five years. The building was finished in a more utilitarian manner by 1900 and the 'bankruptcy line' is said to be seen at the fourth floor.

The equestrian statue of Lord Napier, 1810-90, was moved to its present location at the north end of Queens Gate from its original site in Waterloo Place in 1921. The statue is basically the work of Edgar Boehm but it was finished by Alfred Gilbert after Boehm's death. Its upward slope was to allow for the rise in the road at its original location.

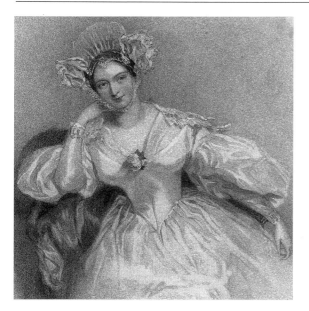

106. Marguerite, the Countess of Blessington.

107. An assembly at a Blessington salon. The guests include Thackeray (bottom left) Bulwer Lytton and Count D'Orsay (standing centre), Daniel Maclise and Charles Dickens (far right).

Story Book Houses

THE GLITTERATI OF GORE HOUSE

Philanthropy, scandal and gastronomy all have a part in the story of Gore House, a homely country villa that became a mansion, the site of which is now occupied by part of the Royal Albert Hall. Built around 1750, its early residents included Admiral Rodney, a hero of the Napoleonic wars but in 1808 it was taken by the philanthropist William Wilberforce. He enlarged it considerably and revelled in the quiet seclusion of its garden, which he described glowingly in letters to friends, 'Three acres of pleasure grounds, as if I were two hundred miles from the great city.' It was here, in his library, that he would deliberate with his many parliamentary friends about measures which led to the abolition of slavery and child labour in the mines and factories.

Wilberforce left Gore House in 1821 and after several short occupations and periods of emptiness it was taken by Lady Marguerite Blessington, one of the most colourful figures in an era rich in such characters, although she was then approaching a portly middle age. An early loveless marriage ended in widowhood that left her free

to legalise a long-standing relationship with the Earl of Blessington. When he too died, of an apoplectic fit during a tour of Europe, she returned to England with her stepdaughter and husband, Count Alfred D'Orsay. Although ten years her junior the Count found his stepmother very interesting and very soon was spending more time in the studio set up for him at Gore House than in his own neighbouring cottage.

Marguerite was then to devote her life 'to bringing people together' and those people included all the great names of her time. She moved, in the words of a contemporary writer, 'almost queen-like in a world of intellectual distinction, reigning over the best circles of London celebrities and reckoning among her most admiring friends the most eminent men in England in every walk of life.'

Among this glittering throng was the exiled Prince Louis Napoleon who graced her salon shortly before his abortive attempt to regain the French throne, promising all present that they would soon be dining with him at Les Tuilleries. He failed and was imprisoned, but on his escape it was at the Countess of Blessington's that a celebration dinner was held. Marguerite was not only a great hostess but also a successful novelist as well as editing an annual *Book of Beauty*. She transformed Gore House into one of the most

elegant homes in London, a fit setting for herself and the dandified Count.

Thomas Carlyle's wife described D'Orsay as being 'as resplendent as a diamond beetle', recording a visit he made to Cheyne Row in 1839 when he arrived in 'a blue and silver coach ... wearing a sky blue cravat, light drab surcoat lined with velvet and two glorious breast pins attached by a chain and enough gold watch chain to have hanged himself in.'

Apart from his lavish spending on clothes, D'Orsay was a gambler, and by 1845 his gambling debts alone amounted to £120,000. These, together with the other large expenses of their lives ended the Blessington period at the house. The bailiffs were called in and the glories of Gore House went under the hammer while its fallen idols fled to Paris. It was said that over 20,000 people attended the sale, which included 2,000 books as well as massive quantities of porcelain, silver plate, paintings, engravings and magnificent furniture. The Countess survived the shame of her financial ruin for only a few months but D'Orsay lasted a little longer, dying three years later having, according to Thackeray, spent his last years 'admiring himself in the most horrible pictures he has painted'.

In 1850 the now vacated Gore House, almost opposite the Crystal Palace rising opposite, caught the eye of the flamboyant French chef, Alexis

108. The gardens of Alexis Soyer's Gastronomic Symposium in 1851.

109. A rear view of Kensington House when it was used as a private lunatic asylum.

Soyer who, while presiding over the kitchens at the Reform Club, created dishes which are still served there today. In a bold but rash step he resigned from the Reform and took Gore House to create a Gastronomic Symposium of All Nations to complement the international spirit of the Exhibition.

Soyer must have delighted the shade of Lady Blessington with his lavish decorative scheme. Each room was given a special theme, such as the Bower of Ariadne and the Celestial Hall of Golden Lilies. The artist, George Augustus Sala, painted exotic murals on the walls of the Great Staircase. Statues were also scattered all over the gardens and shrubberies – where there was room – which was not much as the grounds also had to accommodate a baronial banqueting hall and a 400 feet long pavilion. The venture may have been a social success but it was not profitable, ending up with a loss of £7,000. It closed down at the same time as the Exhibition in October 1851.

Despite his flamboyant nature, Soyer had a serious side. During the 1847 Irish potato famine he set up soup kitchens in Dublin feeding 26,000 people daily. After the failure of the Symposium he produced a *Shilling Cookery Book for the People* with down to earth advice for poor families. His philanthropic nature went even further and with the outbreak of the Crimean War he volunteered

for service in Scutari where he re-organised the hospital kitchens. He produced the sort of food that could be consumed by very sick men and followed this with the invention of a field cooking stove that was still used by troops in 1935.

He returned to England in 1857 with more ingenious inventions such as a sea-going baking dish to add to his earlier 'Magic Coffee Pot' and egg-cooking machine. But the conditions in the Crimea had undermined his health and he died in 1858 the year after Gore House was demolished by the Commissioners.

FIRST RUSSIAN EMBASSY?

Among the wealthiest residents of Kensington at the end of the seventeenth century were the Colbys, a Suffolk family, which had inherited a large area of land south of the Kensington Road opposite the newly-occupied Kensington Palace, an inheritance that was accompanied by law suits for a very long time.

Thomas Colby and his nephew, Philip, had two handsome dwellings, Colby House and Kensington House, next door to each other on the site of what is now the east end of Kensington Court. Both were either rebuilt, enlarged or improved at various times during the first part of the eighteenth century and occupied by a number of notable people. These included at Kensington House from 1746-55, the Russian Ambassador to London, Petr Grigorevich Chernyshev, surely the first instance of Kensington as a diplomatic enclave? A plan of the grounds at that time shows an extensive and well-cultivated ornamental garden with fountains and statues.

From 1756 to 1825 Kensington House, like so many other large houses at the time, was used as a school (*see* p.133), and in 1830 William C. Finch, a member of the Royal College of Surgeons, took it as an asylum. He was already running a similar establishment in Chelsea. The prospectus described 'enlightened moral and mental treatment, a library, billiard room, music and the benefits of religion not neglected, pleasure grounds and comfortable apartments from 21 to 30 shillings a week.' A very different account was given by an ex-patient, Richard Paternoster, who had been forcibly confined there in 1838, first in the *Satirist* and then in a book *The Madhouse System*. Here he wrote of brutal keepers, overcrowding, scanty and bad food, no amusements, books, baths or medical treatment.

The asylum changed hands in 1840 and prospered under the new proprietor. Dr Francis Philp He retired in 1852 but kept the freehold of Kensington House while still residing at Colby House next door. Twenty years later he offered the two houses for sale, both being bought by the amazing Baron Albert Grant who was to build a palace-like house which was never occupied.

THE BARON'S PALACE

It was a huge house in Bath stone, with numerous reception rooms, seven bedrooms all with bathrooms, a music room and billiard room, decorated in the most expensive and ornate manner. The furnishings were the finest available and the art gallery included works by Millais, Frith and Landseer. It was said to have cost £250,000 to build and yet within ten years it was reduced to rubble and its salvageable materials were sold off for about £10,000.

The owner of this vast white elephant was used to juggling with money but this time his act failed. He was born Albert Gettheimer, the son of an English mother and German father. He was brought up in Paris and in London, where his father was an importer and had a French Fancy warehouse in the West End. At the age of twenty five Grant was married and running his own business and although this eventually failed he bounced back to promote numerous companies. In 1865, then living in Addison Road, Kensington, he stood as a Liberal/Conservative candidate for

Kidderminster in the General Election of that year and became an MP. The collapse of the Overend and Gurney Bank, plus the large amount of money his election victory cost, sent him scuttling to Italy, where he seems to have led a sufficiently blameless life to be given the title of Baron by King Victor Emmanuel. On his return to England in 1870 his money-making schemes began in earnest, the general pattern being to promote some speculative venture of little or no worth to unsuspecting shareholders hoping to make a fortune from silver mines or tramways.

It was at the height of this activity that he bought Kensington and Colby Houses to build his own vast mansion. To these he added more land by buying the site of Jennings Buildings and the other notorious 'rookeries' to the west. He paid off those occupants of the hovels who would not go voluntarily and by allowing them to take away

110. Baron Albert Grant, by 'Ape' in 1874.

111. Baron Grant's house in 1877.

what they wished of the buildings saved the cost
of clearance. In the next two years a new Kensington House began to rise in such splendour that
poor old Holland House and its neighbouring
residences seemed shabby relics by comparison.
It had a grand façade, with pink granite Ionic-
columned portico. A central conservatory existed
between the Blue and Yellow Drawing Rooms.
The rest of the ground floor included summer and
winter dining rooms which could be joined to
make a large banqueting area, morning rooms, a
picture gallery, billiard room, library and a ballroom. The central entrance hall, ninety feet wide,
was paved with marble mosaic and had marble
staircases at each end.

The decorations on the walls and ceilings were
a conglomeration of muses, cupids, courtly ladies,
musicians and depictions of classical writers from
Chaucer to Milton in settings of oak, walnut and
plasterwork panelling. The grounds, now vastly
extended, were on the same lavish scale, including
a skating rink, an ornamental lake, an American
bowling alley, an orangery and numerous con-
servatories.

In January 1874 Grant stood again for Parliament, successfully, but this time was very soon
unseated following a petition alleging irregulari-
ties. At the same time some of his dubious financial activities were investigated, his mortgagees
were getting very restive and the builders and
subcontractors working on his mansion were
pressing for payment. In 1877 the empty palace
was put on the market but failed to find a buyer.
It was still vacant a year later and Grant was
hoping that the government might take it to
entertain foreign visitors; another idea was that
it might become a hotel or a club, or even a college.
The club seemed the most likely option on the lines
of Princes or Hurlingham, and the grounds were
opened as an experiment several times during the
summer of 1880. The end came in 1881, with the
decision to sell the site. Demolition began the
following year, parts of the marble staircases being
bought by Madame Tussauds and the iron railings
were sold to Sandown Park racecourse. Grant's
career is uncannily shadowed in the novel *The Way
we Live Now*, which Trollope wrote in about 1873.
In this, one of the central characters is a mid-
European wheeler-dealer with a history of financial failures behind him. He takes a magnificent
house in London, seduces the gullible into unre-
alistic investments, stands for Parliament and is
still living in opulent style at his London house
when his financial pack of cards collapses.

SUBWAYS SERVICES

Another financial acrobat succeeded Grant. He was Jonathon T. Carr who had just sold the attractive but heavily mortgaged Bedford Park Estate and this enabled him to take over the Kensington House lands. In his Kensington Court development Carr combined the appearance of 'Queen Anne' architecture with modern facilities such as a system of subways under the roads to take services such as water, gas and hydraulic power to operate the lifts. The central open space was planted with flowering trees and shrubs rather than the currently popular grass, laurels and privets.

Despite these attractions, progress was extremely slow and Carr, who was also involved with the building of Whitehall Court, was in serious financial troubles. By the time the first houses neared completion Carr had bowed out having just escaped bankruptcy. The minor builders who succeeded him concentrated on small houses and blocks of flats on a more modest scale. Before this, a rich young man had taken one of the most striking houses, no. 1 Kensington Court. He was John Riley, the 25-year-old grandson of the founder of the Union Bank. The exterior was heavily ornamented and the interior was lavishly decorated and furnished. It eventually became part of the Milestone Hotel.

Kensington Court kept its reputation for modern conveniences when the increased demand for electric lighting inspired R.E.B. Crompton, a pioneer of electrical engineering, to convert an old shed into a generating station. A dynamo transmitted direct current on bare copper mains through subways to the houses to charge batteries or accumulators. This system was very quickly expanded to become the Kensington and Knightsbridge Electric Lighting Company in a basement below street level that remained as a sub station until 1985. The old Hydraulic Power Station has been converted into a private house opposite the end of Thackeray Street.

FROZEN IN TIME

Although outwardly indistinguishable from the adjoining houses in Stafford Terrace, the last of the Phillimore developments on Campden Hill, no. 18, is frozen in time. This was the house to which the *Punch* artist, Edward Linley Sambourne, brought his young bride, Marion, in 1874 and which thanks to the devotion of the Sambourne family remains almost exactly as it was a hundred years ago. To walk through its front door is to pass back in time to the social and domestic life of a well-to-do artistic household in Victorian London. When they moved in, Sambourne, aged 30, a 'gentleman apprentice engineer', had only

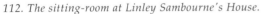

112. *The sitting-room at Linley Sambourne's House.*

113. *Linley Sambourne.*

just been appointed to a junior position on *Punch* where his cartoons and political caricatures were to become a popular feature until his death in 1910. His first political drawings did not appear for over ten years but in 1903 he was appointed successor to John Tenniel. During their long residence the Sambournes' house became a focal point for many writers and artists, especially painters whose works adorned its walls, such as Marcus Stone and Luke Fildes. Regular visitors also included Pinero, Bram Stoker, Rider Haggard and W.S. Gilbert.

Sambourne was also a skilled and enthusiastic photographer and his archive includes over 30,000 prints, all carefully filed in cabinets in his back workroom overlooking the garden. He never acquired a formal studio and did his own processing using the top bathroom!

He worked hard and played hard and his social life sometimes clashed with working hours. The *Punch* weekly meetings on Wednesday gave little time for the meticulously produced woodcuts to be ready by Friday night and he would sometimes work into the small hours by the light of portable gas lamp, with Marion reading aloud from Dickens or Trollope. Almost as interesting as the house is the diary which was kept by his wife, which provides a detailed account of life in Victorian Kensington for three decades. It it was through her granddaughter, Anne, Countess of Rosse, that

the house was preserved in this unique way.

The Sambournes had two children, Roy who remained a bachelor, and Maud, who married Leonard Messel. The Messels' children, Oliver, the theatrical designer and Anne, continued their parents' devotion to the house. Anne, a great beauty in her day was first married to Ronald Armstrong Jones and their son Anthony, Lord Snowdon, married Princess Margaret.

In 1980, Anne, then Countess of Rosse, sold the house to the GLC and on the demise of that body it passed to the Royal Borough of Kensington and Chelsea, although continuing to be administered by the Victorian Society of which the Countess was a founder. It is now open to the public complete with all its treasures.

A CASTLE IN KENSINGTON

One of the most unusual houses in London, but one that very few people except private guests have ever seen inside, is Tower House, in Melbury Road. Built in 1876 by the Victorian architect, William Burges, for his own occupation, it was modelled on a residence of the fifteenth century, with a conical tower, castle-like embrasures and mullioned windows. It also reflects the medieval style of Castell Coch that Burges had created for the Marquess of Bute near Cardiff.

The site belonged, as part of the Holland House Estate, to the Earl of Ilchester. Burges was granted a 90-year lease from 1875 at an annual ground rent of £50 for the first two years and £100 thereafter. From the outside the house is interesting and romantic but it is its interior which really tells a story, each room having a theme from the arts, legends, or nature.

The bronze entrance door was decorated with symbols of the Four Ages of Man and leads into a grand baronial hall where visitors must first step over the mosaic of Burges' pet poodle before reaching the central floor design depicting a labyrinth in which Theseus is slaying the Minotaur. The dining room has a frieze of fairy tale figures but it is hard to look at anything but the striking ceiling decorated with emblems depicting the Sun and the Planets, the Signs of the Zodiac, the Seasons and the Winds. Over the mantelpiece the 'spirit of the house' an ivory-faced goddess with lapis lazuli eyes, was in keeping with the designs that William Burges created in the fashion of Carl Fabergé.

The library on the garden side of the house has stained-glass windows depicting the Muses of Poetry, Music and Architecture while the coffered ceiling features the law-givers, Moses, St Paul, Mohammed, Justinian, Aristotle and Luther. The fireplace, in the shape of a medieval castle, is

114. A ceiling in Tower House.

115. Tower House, saved from demolition, is now in prviate occupation.

fronted by the parts of speech, as figures, presided over by Mistress Grammar, while a frieze below the mantelpiece contains the alphabet. Pictures of birds by Burges' neighbour, H. Stacey Marks, from whom Burges bought seventy at £1.00 each, decorate the bookcase door.

The Drawing, or Music Room, was dedicated to the Fortunes and Misfortunes of Love the chimney piece covered with figures from Chaucer's *Romance of the Rose*. Sadly, Burges did not live long to enjoy the house. He died in 1881 before it was completed, having contracted a chill while driving in an open carriage.

In the 1950s when redevelopment was beginning after the war, there were fears that many old houses of priceless artistic value would be sacri-

ficed. This applied particularly to Tower House, which stood empty for four years from 1962. There were times when, despite efforts by the Kensington and Victorian Societies and John Betjeman, it seemed it might even be demolished.

But it was saved and restoration began in 1966. Further extensive renovations were made when the actor, Richard Harris, acquired the house in 1969. Fortunately the strength of the structure had withstood the damage done by vandals and squatters. Tower House is now in private occupation.

THE ABBEY
Another short-lived fantasy house was The Abbey, built in 1879 for a wealthy stockbroker, William Abbott, who held the lease of the site between Phillimore Walk, Campden Hill Road and Hornton Street. There is no religious significance in the name of the fake castle – it was a pun on the owner's name. The interior was as romantic as its Gothic exterior with castellated walls and towers. The ground floor halls were decorated with statues and scenes from English history, and the stained-glass windows depicted Arthurian legends. Bombing during the last war destroyed the house and the site lay derelict for many years before being used to build the new Central Library, opened in 1960.

116. The main staircase in The Abbey.

117. Palace Green, c.1750.

Millionaires' Row

The name of 'Millionaires' Row' was applied to Kensington Palace Gardens early in its life. One had to be very rich indeed to afford the huge houses built there in the mid 19th century.

In 1838 Queen Victoria decided to extend the kitchen gardens at Frogmore to supply the needs of Windsor Castle. To finance this it was decided to sell off the old Kensington Palace kitchen gardens and orchards on its western boundary. When rumours of this first surfaced, the landscape gardener, John Loudon, protested vigorously in a letter to *The Times* under the pseudonym of 'An Inhabitant of Bayswater'. His protest was unsuccessful and soon plans were in hand for a road running north-south from Bayswater Road to Kensington Road, with a short cross road (now York House Place) connecting it to Church Street. Thirty-three building plots were made available.

The barracks which housed the Palace guards were demolished. Also taken down were two old water towers. One was described by Faulkner as King Henry VIII's Conduit, which was used to relay water to his palace at Chelsea. A mews was

also built at the northern end of the road, of which many people today are unaware.

Sales of the plots were slow. One of the earliest takers was John Marriott Blashfield whose firm made ornamental paving, who leased no less than twenty plots in 1843. Strict rules were laid down as to the type of houses built. They had to be of a standard which would not price them below £3,000. They were to be at least 60 feet back from the road and have ornamental gardens. Their occupants had to be of a superior class. The architectural style was to be 'Italian', which meant that most had towers or belfry-like embellishments, porches and grand columned entrances. There was some doubt about the first house to be built (no. 8 by Blashfield) as it was thought by some to be Byzantine. It was also so large that its first occupier divided it in half. During the last war it was used for the interrogation of spies, after which it was so dilapidated that despite plans to convert it into flats it was demolished in 1961 and luxury flats built on its site. Soon after its construction, Blashfield went bankrupt and returned to ornamental paving.

The Great Exhibition of 1851 revived the fortunes of the enterprise. By 1870 the 'Queen's Road' was known as Kensington Palace Gardens and

118. The southern end of Kensington Palace Gardens.

was at last what the *Illustrated London News* had predicted, 'the most aristocratic neighbourhood', though its titled residents were few. They included the Earl Harrington, owner of the South Kensington estate, who took no. 13, later to become the Soviet Embassy. It is one of the largest houses in the road and after his death in 1862 his widow lived there until 1898. In the 1871 census she had twenty servants – the domestic arrangements included a dairy, laundry, still room, wine room, dung house and dust pit.

The neighbouring house was built by railway entrepreneur Sir Samuel Morton Peto MP. Although large enough to accommodate 28 people, including sixteen servants, it was still not large enough and he built an even grander dwelling next door, selling the previous house to Manchester cotton merchant, Alexander Collie, who spent more money on it before going bankrupt. These two houses are now nos. 12 and 12a, and one is the Royal Nepalese Embassy.

In marked contrast was the first occupant of the very beautiful no. 15, George Moore, a wealthy lace manufacturer and philanthropist who had begun his working life as a £30 a year draper's assistant in Soho. He said he only bought the house to please his wife and, mortified by the extravagance, described it as 'both wicked and aggrandising, mere ostentation and vain show'. The house was remodelled in 1937 for another philanthropist, Sir Alfred Beit, when its internal decoration equalled or surpassed its exterior, the

119. An interior in No. 23 Kensington Palace Gardens.

panels in the dining room at one time containing Murillo's painting of the parable of the Prodigal Son. In the 1970s this house became the Iraqi Embassy.

Other works of art were to be found in no. 11, where the drawing room had a series of canvas panels by Alfred Stevens depicting characters from the *Faerie Queen* and the morning room ceiling was decorated by the same artist. These were regarded as being among Stevens' most important works and it was urged that they should be preserved. The advice was ignored, although sketches for them are still to be seen at the V & A and the Tate Gallery.

From 1868 until his death in 1899, no. 18, one of Charles Barry's paired houses with square towers at each end, was occupied by Julius de Reuter, the founder of the international news agency. He found it too small and added a billiard room and art gallery.

In 1930 the Soviet government acquired the lease of no. 13 from Lady Richardson. This was the first diplomatic arrival and by the 1970s the Soviets had a number of other houses in the road. It was estimated a few years ago that there were over fifty diplomatic residences in Kensington.

120. No. 8 Kensington Palace Gardens.

The west side of Palace Green was not developed until 1903, when more money was needed for gardens at Windsor. Seven fine houses went up between then and 1912.

The three old houses at the southern end of Palace Green date back to the late 17th and early 18th centuries. In 1867 George James Howard bought the lease of no. 1 with the idea of rebuilding, but his plans were condemned as 'inferior, hideous and commonplace'. A new house was eventually built in 1869 by Philip Webb with help from members of the Pre-Raphaelite Brotherhood including Burne-Jones, Morris and Crane. After the First World War it was used as a furniture store by Barker's and after plans to demolish it were defeated, it was converted into flats in 1957.

No. 2 Palace Green (now the Israeli embassy) was leased to William Thackeray in 1860. It was in a very dilapidated condition and although the Queen opposed any new building opposite the Palace he was allowed to build 'the reddest house in town', his daughter saying that her father had thus set the fashion for red brick. 'The house is delightful', Thackeray wrote to a friend. 'I have paid 5,000 on it in two years, out of income, but there's ever so much more to pay. I don't know how much.'

No. 3 was originally occupied by the Clerk of Works at Kensington Palace and prior to that was said to have been the site of the Palace laundry at the time of Queen Anne – old washing boilers were found in its ancient sheds. In 1885 it was bought by Francesco Canziani and his young wife, a portrait painter, Louisa Starr, who had it decorated in the fashion of the time. It was here that their daughter, Estella, grew up and was to live for the rest of her long life as the house gradually became a time capsule of Victorian life. She too was an artist whose pictures of birds and fairies in Kensington Gardens enjoyed several decades of popularity. She was very reclusive, but was a much loved member of the Hammersmith Quaker Meeting. When she died in 1967 the old house was put up for sale and later demolished to build flats.

121. *(Above) No. 13 Kensington Palace Gardens, now the Russian Embassy.*

122. *(Below) Thackeray outside his house at 2 Palace Green.*

123. *(Right) The Canzianis in their garden at Palace Green.*

The Artists' Quarter

If a palette is the collective term for painters it existed for over half century in four acres of Kensington to the west of Holland House. At the height of its popularity practically every house in Melbury and Holland Park Roads was occupied by an artist. Even more remarkable perhaps is that the most famous of them were living in houses built to their own specifications. By the turn of the century the residents included seven Royal Academicians nationally acclaimed for their work, plus dozens of other professional artists occupying studios in the adjacent mews.

So many things are brought about by quirks of fate and this artists' quarter of Kensington is no exception. It was a consequence of the youthful adventures of one of its earliest residents, George Frederick Watts, whose friendships drew to the neighbourhood Frederick Leighton, Val Prinsep, Luke Fildes, William Hamo Thornycroft, Marcus Stone, James Shannon and Holman Hunt.

Watts (1817-1900) had already exhibited at the Royal Academy by the time he was twenty and with prize money won from his success in a competition for designs for the new Palace of Westminster journeyed to Italy. There he was warmly welcomed by the Minister Plenipotentiary, Henry Edward Fox, the fourth Lord Holland, then engaged in a diplomatic career and whose wife Mary Augusta greatly admired his work. He was invited to stay at their homes in Florence and in the Tuscan countryside – a visit intended to be for a few weeks but which lasted three years.

On Watts' return to England he helped the Hollands with the restoration of Holland House and from that was introduced to fashionable society. His circle of friends and admirers grew rapidly and among these was Henry Thoby Prinseps, a wealthy retired East India Company official. When the Prinseps were looking for a London home, Watts persuaded Lord Holland to lease them Little Holland House, then vacant following the death of his aunt, Caroline Fox.

SHARED HOME

Very soon after they moved in Watts was taken ill and the Prinseps nursed him back to health. Once again, a short visit was extended this time, as Mrs Prinsep would laughingly relate, "for thirty years". This was to their mutual benefit as Watts shared their brilliant world of political, literary and artistic society and he in turn gave their talented son Valentine the benefit of his artistic skills.

Watts was fifty before he began to sculpt. His

124. Melbury Road and the corner of Abbotsbury Road, c.1905. The houses on the left were demolished in the 1960s.

whole output was very small compared to his production of over 2,000 paintings, most of which he willed to the nation and now form the Watts Collection at Crompton. His pictures were often melancholy –*The Irish Famine, Found Drowned* etc. – and were not commercially popular but money did not over-concern him. His portraits of the famous of the day won acclaim and brought him rewards when he needed them.

At the age of 47 he married the 16-year-old actress Ellen Terry who had sat for him with her sister. Predictably the union was a failure lasting less than a year and, it is said, was never consummated. In 1867 he was made an RA.

In the early 1870s it was becoming apparent that the now widowed Lady Holland was facing financial problems which could only be met by selling off plots of land from the estate. The lease of Little Holland House was coming to an end and it also stood right in the path of the new Melbury Road. She warned her friends, Watts and the Prinseps, that very soon their home for so many years would have to be demolished.

HUGE STATUES

Watts realised with great sadness that if he had to move the best solution would be to buy one of the plots of land, have his own house built on it and thus remain in the area he loved. Rewarding the Prinseps for their years of hospitality, he bought them a house on the Isle of Wight where their mutual friend, Tennyson, was already living.

His own house, designed for him by his friend, Frederick Pepys Cockerell, had three studios and numerous workshops but even these were not enough to accommodate his very large sculptures. These included the great equestrian statue of 'Hugh Lupus' an ancestor of the Marquis of Winchester, who had commissioned it and arranged for a Percheron horse to be brought over from France as a model.

Frustrated at times by his client's instructions, Watts followed *Hugh Lupus* with a similar work to please himself, the famous *Physical Energy* – 'man as part as creation.' This was much admired by Cecil Rhodes when visiting Watts' studio to sit for his portrait and when Rhodes died not long after, Watts was asked to make a bronze casting of it to mark his grave in Rhodesia. The casting was exhibited at the Royal Academy Exhibition in 1904 but had to stand in the courtyard as it was too big to take into the building. It eventually became the central figure in the Rhodes Memorial on Table Mountain. Other castings stand in Harare and in Kensington Gardens.

Watts remarried in 1886, when he was nearly

125. G.F. Watts in his garden with his vast statue 'Physical Energy'.

seventy, to a Scotswoman, Mary Fraser-Taylor, a working sculptress over thirty years his junior. She changed his austere life style a little by including the occasional steak in his diet of lentils, milk and barley water. He died in 1904, at the age of 87, from the effects of a cold he had caught while working on the statue in his garden. After his death it was Mrs Watts who attended to much of the business of its installation in Kensington Gardens. Transportation once again proved very difficult, with its seven tons having to be pulled by six drays from Burton's Foundry at Thames Ditton.

Little Holland House survived until the end of its lease in 1963 when it was demolished, despite valiant efforts to save it, to build Kingfisher House flats.

THE HIGH VICTORIAN

Distinguished scholarly forebears, a happy childhood and a youth filled with culture and travel, Frederick Leighton (1830-1896) had all the inherited advantages for success. Later in his life, which had been remarkably successful, he said 'Thank heavens I was never clever at anything', believing

126. *Lord Leighton.*

127. *Lord Leighton's studio.*

his success was due to hard work as much as a heaven sent talent.

He was in fact clever at many things apart from his 'High Victorian' art. He was musical, a witty conversationalist, a good friend to famous contemporaries,and held a position in the life of the country well beyond the sphere of his artistic triumphs; he was even a popular figure with the masses through his drawings in the *Illustrated London News*.

The social circle of the 4th Lord Holland during his stay in Italy in 1850s, in which George Watts had become so intimately involved, also included the young Leighton, then a darkly handsome man of twenty who had already travelled widely. Drawn into the life of the English colony he and Watts became good friends despite the disparity in their ages, brought together by their mutual artistic aspirations.

On their return to England both continued to move in the orbit of Holland House. In 1855 Leighton's *Cimabue Madonna*, his first submission to the Royal Academy Exhibition, 'so enchanted Prince Albert that he made me buy it,' wrote Queen Victoria, who paid 600 guineas for it on opening day. The pattern of Leighton's future life was set.

128. The corner of Holland Park Road and Abbotsbury Road in 1898.

Ten years later he became an ARA and decided that it was time he set the seal on his success by leaving his lodgings in Bayswater and setting up a home of his own – a very grand house indeed – much to the concern of his father. In 1866, through his friendship with the Hollands, he obtained a 99-year lease on a plot of their land just west of the old farmhouse in what was to become Holland Park Road. Leighton would tell his friends that he 'lived in a mews' at a time when it was not fashionable to do so and certainly the buildings opposite were mainly stables.

The architect he engaged was another old friend from the Italian days, George Aitchison, although he took an active part in the design himself.

From the outside the house was comparatively modest, in red brick and much smaller than now. It was, of course, the interior on which Leighton lavished so much care and expense, especially the famous Arab Hall created ten years later, an authentic reconstruction based on drawings made in Moorish Spain. The tiles were mainly 17th-century originals brought back from the Middle East by Leighton and friends such as Richard Burton.

Leading figures in the world of interior decoration, including Walter Crane, Ralph Caldecott, Edgar Boehm and William de Morgan, contributed to the house's décor. To all this was added Leighton's own skill as a collector and connoisseur.

Many social occasions were held there, but to discourage visitors from overstaying their welcome there was only one bedroom. There were at least five public areas for entertainment. Contemporary descriptions note splendid carpets hanging from the gallery, flowers in every corner, the pictures of the year standing on easels, lovely women and handsome men, music and singing. Leighton himself had a good tenor voice and frequent guests included Joseph Joachim, the violinist and Sir Charles Hallé, founder of the Hallé Orchestra.

Sure to have been there from the 1870s would be his model, Dorothy Dene, strikingly beautiful, whom he affectionately called 'Little Tee-to-tum.' She was never considered to be his mistress but he took her under his wing, paying for her training as an actress and sending her to Italy when she was ill.

LAST DAYS

His normal daily routine was simple, starting work early, sometimes strolling down the lane to see his friends Watts or Val Prinsep or resting in his leafy garden, where two of his famous statues, *The Sluggard* and *Athlete wrestling with a python*, still stand. The latter was presented to Watts who described it as 'the most beautiful thing he possessed' but he returned it to the house after Leighton's death. Leighton had been made a RA in 1868 and in 1878 became, as forecast long before by Millais, the President of the Royal Academy, as well as receiving a knighthood. In 1886 he became a baronet and was elevated to the peerage in 1896, the only English artist to be accorded this honour. In 1888 he had suffered the first symptoms of heart trouble but he continued his work and travels.

The final heart attack came only a few weeks after he received his peerage. His body was laid out in state at his home before being taken to Burlington House prior to the funeral at St Paul's, his palette and brushes being placed on the coffin. The funeral procession from Piccadilly was escorted by a detachment of the Artists' Rifles of which he, Val Prinsep and many others of the Melbury Road colony had been members, and the pallbearers at the cathedral included John Millais. A wreath of laurels from Queen Victoria was placed on the coffin before the interment in the Painter's Corner, near Wren, Landseer, Turner and Joshua Reynolds. Leighton's estate was willed entirely to his sisters but with the instruction that the entire contents of the house were to be sold and the money donated to the Academy and various art charities. The only remaining item is the chair made by the Royal Workshops at Sandringham with a cover worked by the Princess of Wales.

His sisters generously offered the house to the nation, subject to its maintenance being assured, and a society was formed under the leadership of Mrs Russell Barrington, which maintained it until 1926, when it was transferred to the Royal Borough of Kensington, which purchased the freehold from the Ilchester Estate.

The house suffered bomb damage during the war and was not re-opened until 1951. In 1929 the Perrin Gallery, designed by Halsey Ricardo, a gift from Mrs Henry Perrin in memory of her husband, was added to the east side. After a period of anxiety as to its future, which affected the whole of the 'artists' quarter', Leighton House is now a listed building and open to the public as a museum.

WEALTHY BOHEMIAN

Val Prinsep (1838-1904) was only thirteen when 'Signor', G. F. Watts came to live with his parents at Little Holland House. Probably intended to follow his father's career as an Indian Civil servant, his skill as an artist was soon recognised by Watts who became his mentor. A 'golden boy' over-indulged by his parents, he nevertheless rewarded them by early success. Having toured Italy in company with Edward Burne-Jones he studied at the Atalier Gleyre in Paris, where his fellow students included Whistler and du Maurier, and first exhibited at the Royal Academy in 1862.

He never missed a year after this but even then the early financial rewards would not have enabled him to build himself a house when he was only 24 had he not had parental backing. The architect he chose was Philip Webb, who had designed William Morris's house at Bexley, and the site was one of the new plots leased by the Holland House Estate.

His house in Holland Park Road was built round a large Parisian-style studio. Although the traditional rear entrance for models was installed, Val's happy go lucky nature (he was known as 'the roughs' and prize fighters' pal), ensured that he usually let them in at the front door.

In 1878 he travelled to India to paint the historic picture of the Durbar organised by Lord Lytton to celebrate the dedication of Queen Victoria as Empress of India. The people of India presented the huge painting, 30 feet by 12 feet, to the Queen. This was to be followed by many pictures on Indian themes as well as the great epic story paintings so beloved of the Victorian public. He maintained his bachelor status and bohemian life style until 1884 when he married Florence Leyland, daughter of the wealthy Liverpool ship owner and art patron, Frederick Leyland. Wealthy, socially popular, he also enjoyed success as an author with an account of his visit to India, *An Artist's Journal*, two plays and two novels.

In 1875 when his old mentor, Watts, was planning to build a new home in the area, Prinsep leased him a large part of his garden fronting on to Melbury Road on which to put it.

Prinsep died at the age of 56 in 1904, the same year as Watts. The house that had been much altered to provide more room for family life after Prinseps' marriage became 14 Holland Park Road and in 1948 was converted into flats.

THE BOUNDER

Watts' neighbour at no. 8 Melbury Road was 'that young bounder' Marcus (Apollo Belvedere) Stone (1840-1921) who, when he acquired the 99-year lease of the land from Lady Holland in 1875, was about to become an ARA.

The son of an ARA, Frank Stone, it had been accepted that he would follow in his father's footsteps and under paternal tuition he had exhibited at the Academy by the time he was 19. He had also begun to illustrate some of the books of Charles Dickens, who was one of his father's friends in a circle that also included both Thackeray and Trollope.

Apart from his work as an illustrator which earned him much popular acclaim, his sentimental paintings with historical themes or human stories, *First Love Letter, A Soldier's Return, A*

129. *Marcus Stone's house at 8 Melbury Road.*

130. *Nos 2 and 4 Melbury Road, with the annexe built by Hamo Thornycroft to accommodate his talented family.*

Gambler's Wife, were commercially successful as engravings and reproductions, much in demand at the time. The architect he chose for his new home was the fashionable Norman Shaw. In characteristic red brick and built as an artist's working studio, it still had a quiet homeliness, with domestic comforts. Heated by hot water pipes, the corner fireplaces were to provide the' company of a cheery fire'. This cosiness was somewhat offset by the touch of snobbery which gave the house three gates on to Melbury Road, one for the models, one for servants and one for the family. Stone became a RA in 1886 and died in 1921.

A FAMILY OF SCULPTORS

To the west of his new home Watts had a positive colony of artists in a house built at almost the same time as his own. The sculptor and Watts' contemporary, Thomas Thornycroft, who had been working on the Albert Memorial, had taken two

plots of land. He was to build two studio houses, one for himself and his large family and the other as an investment to let. The Thornycrofts consisted of Thomas and his wife Mary, also a working sculptor, and five children. In addition to William Hamo Thornycroft (1850-1925) there were three daughters, all sculptors and/or painters and another son John, an engineer who became a pioneer in the development of torpedo boats.

As one might imagine, to accommodate such a family the Melbury Road house was a rambling complex of studios, workshops and galleries set around its domestic quarters which reflected the family's love of music, books and good living as well as their capacity for work. It was set in a large and leafy garden where a turntable had been set up to enable huge blocks of marble to be moved.

Elected as ARA in 1881 and a RA seven years later, Hamo was kept busy with commissions as a portrait sculptor and particularly for colonial monuments. When he married in 1885 the house was already feeling the strain of its numerous occupants, so a studio annexe was built next door as no. 2a. The second original house, no. 4, had been let out to Mr & Mrs Barrington, who had been encouraged by Watts to move into the artists' enclave. Mrs Barrington, who considered herself both an artist and writer, was among those who campaigned to preserve Leighton's house and wrote biographies of both Leighton and Watts.

Among Hamo Thornycroft's most famous works are the statue of General Gordon moved from Trafalgar Square to the Horse Guards, the statue of Oliver Cromwell at Westminster and the figure of Coleridge in Westminster Abbey. Every day Londoners see what is considered one of his finest works, the frieze on the outside of the Institute of Chartered Accountants in the City.

Thornycroft was knighted in 1917 and continued working right to the end of his life, listing his recreations as gardening, cycling and trout fishing. His last works included the Luton War Memorial and a statue of Bishop Yearman Biggs in Coventry Cathedral. He died in December 1925 at the age of 75.

BOMBED

The last of the group of the 1870s houses in Melbury Road was the first to go, and the only one to be seriously damaged during the Second World War. This was no. 14, built for the Scottish artist, Colin Hunter (1814-1904) who favoured seascapes, many painted in the Hebrides. In 1879, the Chantrey Bequest bought *Their Only Harvest*. He became an ARA in 1884. He died in 1904 at the age of

63. His house, although including a spacious studio, was intended for family living with a large number of bedrooms and nurseries for the children. Badly bombed it was demolished soon after the war and flats built on the site.

THE FAMILY MAN

While their fathers were busy at their easels the children of Luke Fildes (1843-1927) and Colin Hunter would wave to one another from their nursery windows on either side of Melbury Road. Of all the 'Melbury' artists, Fildes was the family man. His children, all six of them, had the run of his huge and beautiful house no. 11 (now 31) Melbury Road on the corner of Ilchester Place.

Born in Liverpool in 1843 on St Luke's Day, hence his name, Fildes came to London to study at the South Kensington Art Schools in 1863 having won a £50 scholarship.

After working as an illustrator for popular magazines while improving his painting skills he submitted his first entry to the Royal Academy in 1872 to be followed two years later by the famous *Casual Ward,* a queue of down and outs waiting for admission to the workhouse. Achieving in-

131. Luke Fildes' family in their garden.

stant public acclaim it was followed by a series of story pictures including *The Doctor*, the sick-room scene of a physician keeping vigil over a young patient as well as *The Village Wedding*.

In 1874 Fildes decided to build his own house in Melbury Road, also using Norman Shaw as its designer. Shaw congratulated him on having 'ob-tained a delicious site' from Lady Holland and Fildes said his house would 'knock Stone's to bits.'

It was indeed a palace, half as big again as his friend's with a huge studio, ample living room, and a glass house where the children play-acted. He called the house *Woodside* in recognition of its pastoral setting for in those days Nightingale Lane (now Ilchester Place) was a floral byway in which the cows from Holland House pastures, bells tin-kling, came down to be milked twice a day at Tunk's and Tisdall's dairy in the High Street.

'Show Sunday' at the Fildes' was the social event of the art year. The parlour maid counted nearly seven hundred visitors in 1883, dropping a coffee bean into a brass bowl as each visitor came up the grand staircase. In 1887, after painting a portrait of his wife, Fanny, also an artist, Fildes discovered his talent in this new field. From then on por-traiture took over from the earlier popular sen-timental subjects but with equal success, including State Portraits of the King and Queen. King Edward considered Fildes' studio 'one of the finest rooms in London.' Fildes became a RA in 1887 and was knighted in 1906. He lived at Melbury Road for the rest of his life, dying in 1927 at the age of 84.

The house is now occupied by the impresario and film director, Michael Winner, who has played a prominent part not only in its preservation but that of the whole area of the 'Leighton settlement' as it was known in its heyday.

THE TOWER NEXT DOOR
One wonders what the six Fildes' children made of the fairy-tale castle being built next door by William Burges at what is now 29 Melbury Road. Burges had been articled to an architect when he was seventeen and made a special study of the medieval period. Tower House was straight out of a thirteenth century romance (*see* p.99). Across the way from the Fildes' house at the present 47, Walford Graham Robertson (1867-1948), a portrait painter, indulged in the luxury of having a house built for him which he used as a studio and for entertaining clients while he lived in Argyll Road. He was one of the last arrivals in the neighbour-hood, in 1893, and further additions were made to the house in 1912 after he left. For several years he shared the studio with the young Scots impres-sionist painter, Arthur Melville, until his death in

1904. Robertson was also the author of several books and plays. The building was converted into flats in 1948.

THE TILED HOUSES
At the same time, the engineer, Sir Alexander Meadows Rendel, commissioned Halsey Ricardo to design the pair of semi-detached houses faced in oxblood red tiles at nos. 55 and 57 Melbury Road. Ricardo explained these in *The Builder*. He hoped that the fire glazed bricks would 'be proof against the disintegrating forces of London air... wind proof and rain proof and only need washing down ... virtually indestructible.' One of the houses was taken by Sir Ernest Debenham who later com-missioned Ricardo to build him a similar house in less lurid colours at the north end of Addison Road.

Sir James Jebusa Shannon (1862-1923) did not lease the land for his studio, next door to Leighton's in Holland Park Road, from the Earl of Ilchester but from the Tisdalls, the Earl's tenants at Holland House farm. Shannon had a studio built next door and although the farmhouse core remained the exterior was completely altered. James Shannon was amongst the most famous portrait painters of his time. Born in America of Irish parents, he came to London when he was sixteen. He exhib-ited regularly at the Royal Academy from the age of 19 to the year before he died. He became RA in 1909 and was knighted in 1922. The house was divided in two after his death to become 2 and 2a Holland Park Road.

PHIL THE FUNNY MAN
For a decade or so at the end of the Victorian era, Phil May (1864-1903) chronicled the humour of life through his art in the pages of *Punch* and other periodicals. During much of that time he was living in Holland Park Road, firstly in 1892 at no. 7, then at Rowsley House, now no. 20.

Even in that short time his neighbours must have been aware of his eccentricities, just as the editors who employed him recognised his brilliance enough to endure his unreliability. Born in Leeds, his father died when he was nine and he had a very limited education in Board schools. At 13 he joined a travelling theatre company taking small parts, designing costumes and painting scenery. For a while he thought he would be a jockey and he affected a horsey look all his life wearing breeches, checked jackets and gaiters. Coming to London to seek his fortune he was penniless until befriended by a photographer who published some of his theatrical sketches. In 1885 he married a

132. Phil May and his wife at Rowsley House, 20 Holland Park Road.

young widow and emigrated to Australia where he worked successfully on humorous drawings for the *Sydney Bulletin*.

He was living in Holland Park Road when he was appointed to *Punch* and his first work appeared on 14 October 1893 – his initials are on the famous *Punch* table between those of Thackeray and du Maurier. His drawings, like so many in *Punch*, were more than amusing trivia, being a commentary on the social history of the time. Based on class contrasts, the tramp and the toff, maids and mistresses, as well as the news vendors, cockney traders, boot blacks, road sweepers and drunks, of which his own diet of whisky and cigars provided a personal experience.

His life style eventually caught up with him and he died in debt at the age of 39.

The Pre-Raphaelite, William Holman Hunt (1827-1910) spent the last ten years of his life at 18 Melbury Road. His widow continued to live there for many years, making melancholy pilgrimages to St Paul's to visit his tomb and study his famous painting *The Light of the World*. The house was later turned into flats.

DEMOLITION THREAT

Over thirty years ago Kensington's artists' quarter was the subject of a battle between the London County Council with the Kensington Society versus Kensington Council and the Holland House Parways estate. The LCC wanted to put a preservation order on Leighton House and six houses in Melbury Road, including those once occupied by Watts, Stone and Fildes as well as Tower House.

The LCC and the Kensington Society presented their case at a Public Enquiry with support from the London and Victorian Societies. Sir Albert Richardson, who described the group of houses as part of the national heritage, presented the Society's case at the Enquiry. The fear was expressed that the Council's unwillingness to place a Preservation Order on Leighton House suggested that it could be demolished for future development. Apart from 6 Melbury Road, Watt's house, the Inspector recommended the confirmation of the Preservation Order but it did not receive ministerial confirmation. However all the buildings, except no. 6 which was demolished, were subsequently listed.

In later years concern was expressed over the condition of nos. 7-13 Melbury Road, houses less important than their illustrious neighbours but still part of the general ambience of the area. Objections were successful and the houses have now been restored with modern interiors.

The New Town

'It is all very clean and neat and astonishes visitors who a few years ago beheld scarcely a house on the spot.' This is how Leigh Hunt described Kensington New Town, which from about 1839 to 1855 was built on open land east of Victoria Road. But unlike many developments of the day which are boringly uniform, the houses in streets such as Canning Place, Victoria Grove and Launceston Place are pleasingly varied, probably due to the large numbers of small builders who were involved in their construction. The residents were somewhat lower perhaps on the social scale, but many had distinguished artistic reputations such as the sculptor Alfred Stevens, at 7 Canning Place, and the painter, Samuel Palmer, at 6 Douro Place, 1851-61.

In 1881 *Suburban Homes in London* wrote that the area was noted for being 'inhabited by artists of high standard, its villas are certainly beautiful miniatures in themselves. Palmer's son saw it somewhat differently, writing that his father's new home was 'a hideous little semi-detached house with a prim little garden at back and front and ample opportunity for profiting from the next door neighbour's musical proclivities.'

Henry Newbolt, the patriotic poet of *Drake's Drum* and similar verse, found his house, at 14 Victoria Road from 1889 to 1898 small 'but not dark or cramped.' Much later, George Robey dwelt in no. 10 from 1926 to 1932. 52 Victoria Road, Eldon Lodge, was built in 1851 for the painter of dogs and horses, Alfred Hitchen Corbould, professor of drawing and painting to Queen Victoria's children. In 1875, the architect, William Burges, was toying with the idea of living here but changed his mind in favour of Melbury Road where he built Tower House.

The developers of Kensington New Town were John Inderwick, importer of tobacco, who had already been busy in the Palace Gate area, and the son of another merchant, Howell Leny Valloton, whose family fortune came from haberdashery and fancy goods. His father had acquired land in the vicinity at the end of the eighteenth century.

The houses had bad drainage problems until the Metropolitan Board of Works carried out a general sewage improvement scheme for all London. In 1843 a house in Victoria Road was said to have water and sewage rising half way up the joists in the kitchen floor and Inderwick made his own temporary cess pit rather than pay for a new sewer to be constructed.

133. Victoria Road, c.1905.

VICTORIA ROAD, KENSINGTON, W.

134. Anxious passengers for the airship.

Despite its normal tranquillity, the district must have experienced considerable excitement in 1855 when 'the dockyard of the Royal Aeronautical Society' in Victoria Road, opposite Kensington Gardens, became the first 'London Airport'. The announcement was made that the Eagle 'the first aerial ship' which was 160 foot long, 50 feet high and 40 feet wide, manned by a crew of seventeen experimental sailors, would leave for Paris. It was described 'as a stupendous first rate man-of-war, containing 2,400 yards of oil silk on a 75-foot frame, with a six-foot wide cabin suspended in the centre by ropes.' It was to be steered by an immense rudder and four flappers. Future voyages were planned to Vienna, Berlin and St Petersburg but actually the dirigible never left the ground and provided comedians with material for months.

The south-west corner of the estate received a severe shake up when in 1860 construction of the Metropolitan Railway began and some new houses had to be demolished in Stanwick Road and Kelso Place.

One of the last open spaces to succumb to building was the Paddock, once the headquarters of the Kensington Lawn Tennis Club, which in 1887 became Kensington Court Gardens.

For over a decade, Prince of Wales Terrace, the enclave of twenty-two houses off Kensington Road between Kensington Court and De Vere Gardens has been a source of anxiety for conservation and amenity societies. The properties became derelict while development plans were proposed and abandoned, a situation only recently resolved with the rebuilding behind the original facades and the retention of the Prince of Wales motifs.

The Terrace was erected in the 1860s on the site of Madeley House, the home for fifteen years of the Victorian tycoon, William Hoof, who made a fortune from railway building, particularly on the Brighton line. 'A large house in the cottage style', it dated from the beginning of the nineteenth century, a previous occupier being Sir John Scott Lillie, a friend of Hoof and a co-speculator in the Kensington Canal. Hoof died in 1855 leaving the house to his widow, who collapsed and died of shock only hours after her husband. The house was sold, and was shortly afterwards demolished.

The large terrace houses which replaced it had zinc baths on the third floor, water closets on the landings, eleven bedrooms and a hallway heated by hot water coils. Needless to say they were increasingly sub-divided in modern times, one becoming a hotel.

BUILDING ON THE NURSERY

Although Grimwood's Kensington Nursery had closed down in 1847 and the Hippodrome ended its tenure in 1852, it was twenty years or more before the site they occupied was available for development on the same scale as the New Town. The last nurseryman to run the business was Richard Foress, a landscape gardener and architect, although the Grimwoods still held the freehold. In 1848 John Inderwick secured a lease of part of the land fronting the Kensington Road, in order to erect a terrace of nine houses with shops below, called Craven Place. The District Surveyor criticised these as being 'built in a slight and hardly safe manner.' On the south side of the site there were two cottages in large gardens that within about 25 years were replaced by Laconia and De Vere Mews. Craven Place was equally short lived. The delay in the whole development was caused by the emigration of the Grimwood family, which caused a lot of complications, even when they were willing to sell the freehold.

The main development, De Vere Gardens included some very large houses. Nos. 28 and 30 had eighteen bedrooms each. No. 6 was taken by a wealthy Australian merchant, Sir Daniel Cooper, who had it fitted out with stained glass by Walter Hensman. Early residents included Robert Browning (1888-9) at 29 and Henry James, who had 'a chaste and secluded flat' in one of the first houses to be changed into this 'modern' form of residence, De Vere Mansions West. Other occupants were the Marquess of Carmarthen and John Hennicker Heaton MP, the Commissioner for New South Wales, who reflected the growing popularity of the area with those with colonial connections. The residents often employed distinguished artists, such as Halsey Ricardo and Walter Stokes, to embellish their already opulent homes. The houses were, however, slow to sell and in 1874

only four out of the thirty built were occupied.

An acrimonious dispute arose over the site of what is now the De Vere Hotel. Instead of one fine house on the corner of Kensington Road which the local residents thought would set off the neighbourhood, the developers produced 'three barns.' The argument was so serious that it went to the House of Lords, which gave judgement to the builder, although he had by then gone bankrupt. In the 1880s many of the very large houses became flats or hotels, either by conversion or purpose built. In 1897 the 'barns' were remodelled as the De Vere Hotel, with an iron and glass porch designed by Walter Groves and some winged lions by Alfred Drury.

Large Victorian houses were usually accompanied by a mews development in which horses and carriages were kept. As cars became fashionable these properties became redundant and were converted to other uses. De Vere Mews was used until 1974 by the Civil Service Riding Club, the horses being accommodated on the first floor, approached by a ramp. One of the first mews to be converted to residential use was Laconia Mews, changed in the 1920s to De Vere Cottages.

135. The Civil Service Riding Club.

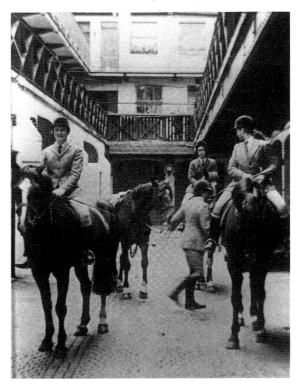

136. *Brompton Park House, the home of Henry Wise, with the 1862 International Exhibition building (demolished in 1864) in the background*

The Garden People

THE KING'S PLANTSMAN

The story of Henry Wise and his partner, George London, mostly belongs to Brompton but Wise's involvement in the gardens of Kensington Palace (*see* p.120) gives him a role in the history of central Kensington. His home, Brompton Park House, where he brought up a family of ten children, ended up as part of the first South Kensington Museum until demolished in 1899.

In 1686 he joined the celebrated Brompton Park Nursery which John Bowack described in his *Antiquities of Middlesex* in 1705 as being famed all over the kingdom. 'Kept in extraordinary order. A great number of men are constantly employed, the stock seems almost incredible if we believe those that affirm that if several plants in it are valued at a penny a piece they would amount to above £40,000.'

John Evelyn, the diarist, also paid tribute to them in his introduction to *The Compleat Gardener*, saying that gain was not their only objective but they 'endeavoured to improve themselves in the mysteries of the profession.' They also 'under-

stood what best to plant and how to disperse and govern the plants according to situation.'

Before the importation of foreign plants became commonplace, evergreens played a large part in English gardens and the Long Greenhouse at Brompton Park was an important part of Wise's work. When George London died, Wise leased the garden to two of his employees. The nursery was by then much enlarged and also included 17 acres at Kensington Gore and 11 acres on the Thurloe Estate.

THE PINEAPPLE SIGN

For a century or more the sign of the pineapple stood over a bow-fronted shop at the corner of what is now De Vere Gardens. This was the nursery of the Grimwood family, a business founded in 1710 by Robert Furber. When Furber died in 1756 his assistant John Williamson succeeded him and it remained in his family until 1783 when it was taken over by Nathaniel Grimwood who also had a shop in Arlington Street, Piccadilly, where his pineapple sign was well known.

The nursery was passed on to William Malcolm, a tenant, because John Desse Grimwood, great

137. *Grimwood's Nursery. The pineapple sign can be seen over the shop.*

grandson of Nathaniel had married a Chilean lady and was living in South America. At this time the business was a large affair. When, in 1843, the property was passed in trust to seven children in Chile, the legal complications were such that the site lay sterile for more than thirty years until it was sold and became De Vere Gardens.

THE RADICAL RIDER

The radical politician and journalist, William Cobbett, was well into middle age when he moved into a cottage at the rear of Scarsdale House off Kensington High Street in 1820. It was from here that he set off on his famous 'Rural Rides'.

Born in 1762, he served in the Army in his young days, including a spell in Canada. Shocked by Army corruption, he returned to England and, inspired by Tom Paine, left for America. There, despite his republican leanings he was regarded as an Anglophile and his newspaper, *Porcupine's Gazette*, incurred an expensive libel action. On his return to England he was hailed as a patriot, his independent newspaper carrying the slogan 'Fear God and Honour the King.' This popularity was short lived. Before long his radical views put him

out of favour, although his famous *Political Register* ran from 1802 until his death in 1835 with only a short break. During this time he was fined £1000 and spent two years in Newgate, having been convicted of seditious libel for his attack on flogging in the Army. After farming again, this time in America, he came to Kensington and leased a plot extending down Wrights Lane which he described as being 'walled in from the roads and distinct from all houses, with a nice garden and four acres of rich land for cows and pigs.'

He also developed a seed farm, specialising in American imports such as maize, and grew saplings. He claimed that his stock consisted of more than a million seedling forest trees and shrubs and three thousand young apple trees. He also found room for 'five fine cows and a pigeon house to hold a hundred pairs, pigs in a sty and a most abundant and fruitful garden.' In an outbuilding he continued to print *The Political Register*.

Cobbett continued to live at Kensington through the period of his 'Rural Rides' around England. In these he wrote about the places and the people he met, spiced up with his own views. These were perhaps the happiest years of his life. In 1827 he bought a larger plot of land at Barn Elms, Barnes,

138. William Cobbett.

139. Princess Alice planting a cherry tree in the garden of Kensington Palace to celebrate Tree Festival Week, in 1951.

but continued to live at Kensington until elected for Parliament in 1831, when he moved to Surrey. The cottage, where he hung a grid iron forged by his supporters to symbolise his opposition to Peel's Bank Bill in 1819, became part of the candle factory (see pp. 72-73). This and the land were all swallowed up in the 1860s by the railway and its sidings.

CELEBRATING WITH FLOWERS

When plans were made to celebrate the Coronation of the present Queen in 1953, a group of local residents decided that flowers would be a better decoration than flags and bunting. The Brighter Kensington Garden Scheme was inaugurated with an annual contest in which residents could enter anything from a window box to a garden square. The patron in the early days was Princess Alice, Countess of Athlone, a granddaughter of Queen Victoria, then living at Kensington Palace and a keen gardener. The scheme, run voluntarily, now includes Chelsea and continues in its 45th year.

MEMORIAL GARDENS

When Princess Alice died in 1980 a Memorial Fund was set up by the Kensington Society and in 1981 an avenue of beech trees was planted in front of Kensington Palace in her memory. A garden was also created by the Society in the forecourt of the new Civic Centre. This includes a Myrtle grown from a cutting of the bush from which a sprig was cut for Queen Victoria's wedding bouquet.

In 1952 the Council converted the St Mary Abbots churchyard into a public garden of rest. This peaceful oasis, with gravestones around the walls and planted with shrubs and roses, is much appreciated by workers and shoppers.

In 1991 another Memorial Garden was opened, this time on a derelict site of surplus land left after rebuilding on the old Town Hall site. This was a tribute, also by the Kensington Society, to their late President, the architectural expert and author, Alec Clifton-Taylor.

Kensington Gardens

Before it became a palace Nottingham House was not without its garden delights, although on a smaller scale. Its owners, three generations of the Finch family, had survived the hazards of the Civil War, and despite their dreary dispositions had added to their social status and prosperity. Daniel Finch, who sold the house to William and Mary, was known as 'Dismal Daniel' or 'Don Dismallo'.

Queen Mary's desire to please her Dutch husband changed the romantic Italianism of the gardens to the formal geometric patterns fashionable in late 17th-century Holland, based on military fortifications, and planted with low hedges of box and yew. She employed George London and Henry Wise, the famous gardeners of Brompton Park Nursery, to do this work. London had been head gardener to Henry Compton, the great gardening Bishop of London at Fulham Palace but his work now took him frequently out of London. So it was Wise who was mainly responsible for the planning and planting of the evergreens for which the nursery was famous in the days before more exotic plants could be imported

from abroad. Sadly, Mary died within five years of her arrival at Kensington and her sister Anne, who hated the smell of box, soon had the hedges pulled up and many changes made.

Although Anne was there only for twelve years she managed a large number of changes and innovations. Within a few weeks of her arrival she wrote to her friend, Sarah, Duchess of Marlborough, that the Kensington garden 'could be a very pretty place if the place were well kept but nothing can be worse.' She promptly dismissed Lord Portland as keeper of the Royal Palace Parks and Gardens and gave Henry Wise full responsibility.

She installed The Alcove, a feature designed by Christopher Wren, which seats at least twelve people on a curved bench, at the south end of Dial Walk. This was removed to the other side of the gardens, near Bayswater Road, in 1857.

It was Henry Wise who drew up the first plans to change the course of the Westbourne river, which meandered southwards across the grounds through a series of small lakes. His intention was to make a 'long water' and a pond near the Palace, but neither came to fruition in Anne's lifetime. When later constructed they materialised as the Serpentine and the Round Pond. Wise was, however, able to complete a garden for Anne on the north-east side of the Palace, although none of it remains.

140. *A Plan of Kensington Gardens, drawn by John Rocque, 1756.*

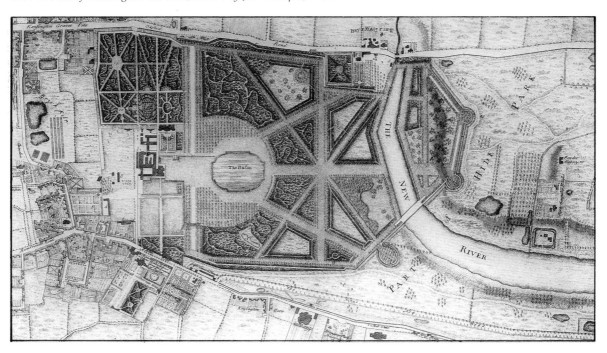

141. *Entrance to Kensington Palace in the eighteenth century.*

142. *Mrs Lacy, attendant at St Gover's Well, in the 1880s.*

GARDENING QUEEN

George I's daughter-in-law, Caroline of Anspach, was passionate about gardens, and responsible for much at Richmond and Kew. She came to Kensington in 1727 at the age of 42. Anne had already extended the cultivated area of the old Nottingham House grounds and Caroline added many more acres, though none from Hyde Park which, well into the late eighteenth century, remained as a large open space in which deer roamed and troops were occasionally stationed.

Henry Wise's partner, Charles Bridgman, became Royal Gardener and advanced the plans for the Serpentine and Round Pond. Two hundred workmen constructed a dam across the Westbourne Valley and hundreds of tons of soil were transported to form a mound on the south-east side. At the same time over a hundred trees were moved.

In 1726 the 'bason [sic] next to the snailery was to be enlarged for Tortices and to be raised so as to hold water 30 feet deep with a fence between the snailery and the Tortice place.' One can only speculate as to whether these creatures were intended for the Palace kitchens. The 'tortices' were a gift to the Queen from the Doge of Genoa who also gave her some red squirrels.

By 1754 Kensington Gardens was completed

much as they are today – only the Serpentine bridge had to wait for nearly a century. By 1733 the Gardens were open to the public on Sundays when the Court was at Richmond, although the rules of admission were strict as regards dress and demeanour. No silk neckties were allowed, nor breeches without boots. The gatekeepers dressed themselves in green livery and were the adjudicators as to who should be admitted, automatically excluding soldiers, sailors and servants. In 1763, James Boswell said it was 'delightful of the King to keep such walks so near the metropolis open to his subjects'.

Public admission increased once the Palace was unused as a home for the monarch. By 1820 Thomas Faulkner wrote that they were now open every day. 'The great south walk leading to the Palace is crowded on Sunday mornings in spring and summer with a display of beauty and fashion... and affords a spectacle not to be equalled in Europe.' A popular attraction in the 1870s was St Gover's Well, about 150 yards from the south end of the Broad Walk and now covered over. Its waters were supposed to possess medicinal qualities and a Mrs Lacy was given the right to sell it for a penny a glass. But in 1875 it was decided that the water was unwholesome and it was replaced by a drinking fountain.

Henry Wise's imaginative use of the Westbourne river had not taken into account its future role as a sewer. In 1849, a year of a cholera outbreak, a meeting held in the Cadogan Institute in Sloane Square, drew attention to its filthy state and foul stench. The river was drained and dredged but the problem returned and in 1858 another attempt was made using lime, but this only had the effect of bringing dead fish and eels to the surface. The evil was finally removed when the sewer was diverted underground in 1860. At the same time, the pool at the north end, which in Caroline's time had been a cascade over stones but had deteriorated into a dirty duck pond, was removed and the area made into an Italian garden with fountains and filtering basins. Nearby is the first of the Gardens' many commemorative monuments, the statue of Edward Jenner by Walter Calder Marshall, originally placed in Trafalgar Square.

143. The Peter Pan statue in Kensington Gardens, by Sir George Frampton.

THE STATUES

The most famous statue, of course, is that of Peter Pan by Sir George Frampton. It was set up in secret during the hours of darkness on 3 April 1912, as if brought by the fairies that clamber around its base. Their heads, with those of attendant rabbits and squirrels, are polished by the hands of generations of children. The figure of Peter was said to be based on the six-year-old Michael Llewellyn Davis, one of the brothers who inspired J.M. Barrie to write his immortal story. Not everyone admired the statue. The author, Wyndham Lewis, described it as 'the sickly and dismal spirit of that terrible book'.

Ivor Innes' *Elfin Oak*, at the north end of the Broad Walk in the children's playground, was carved from an oak stump from Richmond Park. It was restored in the 1960s by Spike Milligan and today, sadly, has to be protected in a metal cage.

There are inevitable memorials of the Empire. These include G.F. Watts' gigantic *Physical Energy* to the east of the Round Pond, a replica of the memorial to Cecil Rhodes on Table Mountain in South Africa. A little to the north is the red granite obelisk to the African explorer, Captain Speke. In 1985 *The Arch*, a 19-foot high sculpture by Henry Moore, was erected on the east side of the Serpentine.

Princess Louise's statue of her mother in coronation robes looks serenely towards the Round Pond despite some modern indignities, such as the removal of her wedding ring finger, since replaced, and her sceptre which was recovered from the bottom of the Round Pond when it was cleaned in 1970.

Lesser known commemoratives are the two sheltered seats on the Broad Walk provided by the Silver Thimble Fund. This little known charity was founded in 1915 by Miss H.E. Hope Clarke in aid of the sick and wounded of the First World War, raising money by the sale of silver thimbles. The scope of the organisation grew to include antique treasures and over thirty years raised money for air ambulances and a launch. The seats in Kensington Gardens, dedicated to soldiers and sailors, have recently been restored.

Memorials of a different kind are found in the Pets' Cemetery just behind the Victoria Lodge. The first interment here took place in 1880, when the Duke of Cambridge was the Park Ranger. His wife's dog was run over just outside the Victoria Gate and was buried here. After that three hundred deeply loved pets, such as 'Wobbles – faithful friend of Hilda and Lily Hanbury', have joined him. The last interment was in 1915 and the cemetery is now closed to the public.

In more recent times two small statues have been added, both with animal connotations. In 1961 the friends of the actor Esme Percy, who had recently died, organised an appeal in his memory to provide a dogs' drinking fountain. At first it was suggested that the dog on the memorial should be a replica of his own spaniel, but this was changed to a mongrel 'embodying the quintessence of universal dogginess'. The sculptor, Sylvia Gilley, used a Lakeland Terrier but altered its appearance to suggest 'decidedly mixed antecedents'.

The other statue of two bear cubs by Kenneth Keeble Smith was erected in 1939 to commemorate the eightieth anniversary of the founding of the Metropolitan Drinking Fountain and Cattle Troughs Association. The figures were stolen but replaced by a replica in 1967.

THE TREES

The first big tree planting in the Gardens was carried out by Charles Bridgman in 1734 with the 'Great Bow', a semi-circle of elms to the east of the Round Pond, said to have replicated the disposition of troops at the Battle of Blenheim. More elms were added along both sides of the Broad Walk. When, in the 1950s, these were said to be diseased, a great controversy broke out over their removal. It was suggested that the real reason for their felling was to provide an emergency airfield to evacuate the royal occupants of the Palace.

In the years that followed 500 trees were lost to Dutch elm disease and were replaced by limes and maples. In 1988-9 the Kensington Society helped to raise money to replace trees lost in the 1987 hurricane. Since the young Queen Victoria played here as a child many generations of children have passed under the hooped entrance from Palace Green, said to be the height of the queen and proving that she really was very small. Until the 1920s an old lady sat here selling balloons and paper windmills. At about the same time, in York House Place, an 'ex-soldier' sat beside a display of dollshouse tables and chairs, modelled from bone and upholstered in red and blue velvet.

Although the Round Pond is associated with little boys fishing for stickle-backs and sailing wooden boats, it is the headquarters of the very serious Model Yacht Sailing Club, with model craft worth many hundreds of pounds.

The attractive sunken garden to the north east of the Palace was created in 1909 as a model of that produced by Henry Wise for Queen Anne two hundred years earlier. The openings in the tunnel of pleached limes reveal the central pool with its antique lead cisterns and the surrounding flower beds, which are kept perpetually colourful.

Public maps of Kensington Gardens do not

144. The Model Power Boat Club Regatta in the 1960s, at the Round Pond.

include the intimate names of paths and routes used by those working there such as the Soldiers' Walk, Peacock Walk, Snobs Crossing and Old Pond Walk, Nanny's Corner and Policeman's Walk.

Sheep grazed the Gardens until the Second World War, acting as organic lawn mowers and becoming quite complacent about dogs.

Also included in Bridgman's plans was the Queen's Temple in the south-east corner of the Gardens now incorporated in Temple Lodge. The Tea Rooms near Albert Gate, now rebuilt as the Serpentine Gallery, were a fashionable venue in Edwardian days when uniformed waiters served ladies at open air tables. Not so far away was the bandstand where Guards Bands played military music every afternoon and evening. Early in 1993 the timber floor of the bandstand was skilfully restored by a Thames boat builder who laid narrow oak planks like a timber deck. Performances are still given at weekends.

Just outside the Queens Gate entrance to the Broad Walk is one of London's few remaining cabmen's shelters which were instigated by Lord Shaftesbury in 1874 to provide good wholesome refreshments at moderate prices as an alternative to the drivers using pubs. This shelter has been preserved by the Heritage of London Trust.

145. *St Barnabas church in 1836.*

More Pews

ST BARNABAS

In 1825, Kensington Vestry decided that the parish church no longer met the needs of the growing population, both to the west and south. Under the Church Building Act, intended to make up for the lack of church building in the preceding war years, Kensington was granted £10,000 towards the building of two chapels of ease. Any additional expenditure was to come from a local church rate.

Lord Holland, who was a Vestryman, offered a site in Addison Road and Lewis Vulliamy, a member of the Swiss clock-making family, was appointed architect for what was to be called St Barnabas. His design was highly reminiscent of King's College Chapel, Cambridge. It was built to accommodate 1,330 people, of which about 800 were in rented pews. But it cost more than the estimate owing to the marshy nature of the soil derived from the old 'moats' or fish ponds of Holland House. It had no tower but there is one bell in the north-west corner turret. In 1909 the east end of the church was remodelled and extended by fifteen feet with a grant made by the owners of Oakwood Court flats as compensation for loss of light and air caused by their new buildings.

Originally St Barnabas was intended as a Low

Church, more for sermons and hymns than sacraments. As a chapel of ease, it was ministered by a perpetual curate rather than a vicar, the first being John Pitman, in 1829, who was also Domestic Chaplain to the Duchess of Kent, mother of Princess Victoria. In 1856, St Barnabas was made a separate parish and Francis Hessey, who had been headmaster at Kensington School, became vicar. His successors have included a number of remarkable churchmen such as the 1939-1945 wartime incumbent, the Rev. William Montgomery Bell, who combined his spiritual duties with stoking the boiler and serving as an air raid warden.

In the 1960s the London Boy Singers, founded by Benjamin Britten, had their headquarters at St Barnabas under the church's choirmaster and organist, Alan Doggett. He was much involved with Andrew Lloyd Webber in the early pop oratorio *Joseph and the Technicolour Dreamcoat*. Shortly before his untimely death in 1978 Doggett and the Boy Singers were presenting another work, *Jason and the Golden Fleece*.

St Barnabas reflects its parish by its many connections with art, music and literature. John Byam Shaw, the artist and illustrator who opened the Byam Shaw Art School on Campden Hill in 1910, was first a choirboy and then a sidesman while living at Addison Road from 1905 to 1919. The stained-glass window depicting St Cecilia and St Margaret is his work and there is a memorial to him on the wall of the north nave.

In 1864 St Barnabas was the scene of the wedding between the 57-year-old G.F. Watts and the very young actress Ellen Terry, a short-lived union. Although a churchwarden of St Stephen's, Gloucester Road, the poet, T.S. Eliot, married his second wife, Esme Valerie Fletcher, at St Barnabas in February 1957.

In recent years, the church, which has seen various phases of liturgy from evangelical Anglican to High Anglican, has become one of the churches 'planted' by the Toronto Experience congregation of Holy Trinity, Brompton, and attracts huge congregations to charismatic services.

In 1854 the Vicar, Francis Hessey, decided to build a temporary church in Warwick Gardens to accommodate those unable to get into the crowded St Barnabas, where congregations averaged 1,400 on Sundays. This became a church hall and is now used by the New Apostolic Church.

OTHER NEW CHURCHES

John Sinclair was appointed Vicar of St Mary Abbots in 1842 and devoted much energy to building new churches in his parish. One was Christ Church, which began as a chapel of ease in 1850 when Kensington New Town was being developed between Victoria Road and Kensington Road. The site, in Victoria Road, was donated by Howell Valloten and the architect was Benjamin Ferrey.

St Philip's, Earls Court Road, had its beginnings in 1842 when a room was taken at the corner of Warwick and Pembroke Gardens as a chapel for the local poor population. However, when it was replaced with a permanent structure the site chosen was much closer to the new squares of Edwardes and Pembroke than to the alleys near the new railway. The freehold was bought for £260 and the St Barnabas curate, Joseph Claxton, paid for half its building costs of £6,500, the rest being raised from private donations, including one of ten shillings made as a thank offering for the discontinuance of the Sunday band in Kensington Gardens! The architect was a well-known Midlands church designer, Thomas Johnson, who was also Claxton's father-in-law. The consecration was on 6 May 1857.

Claxton also paid for the enlargement of the church to match the 'magical rapidity' with which the population grew. Originally, a congregation of 1000 had been envisaged but room for three or four hundred more was achieved by widening the nave and pushing out the south transept.

When Claxton died in 1877 a new vicar, Walter Pennington, who found it hard to exist on the pew rents, succeeded him. He was much put out by

a proposal to build another church south of Cromwell Road and tried to obtain compensation for the effect this would have on his income. This was condemned by his opponents as a 'shameful sale of spiritualities' and they declared him to be 'a disgrace to his sacred office'. He was, however, said by his many friends to be kind hearted and generous and very good at obtaining theatre tickets at Drury Lane!

A POET'S CHURCH

Dwarfed by modern hotels and old Italianate terraces, St Stephen's, Gloucester Road, tucked into the corner of Southwell Gardens, is probably best known today for its association with T. S. Eliot who served as a churchwarden for many years.

It was built in 1866 for a large and fashionable congregation. The original plan included a high tower but this never materialised. In its early days the liturgy was that of Low Anglicans but over the years it moved towards Anglo-Catholicism and in 1890 the vicar, the Rev. Lord Victor Seymour, considering the décor 'unseemly', called in G.F. Bodley to recommend changes and some major alterations were carried out.

In 1996 St Stephen's was in the news when its vicar, verger and 34 of its congregation, left to join the Roman Catholics over the issue of women priests in the Church of England.

IN MUSEUMLAND

A church was built to serve the elegant houses and mansion blocks which surrounded 'Museumland'. Knightsbridge Chapel, once renowned as a venue for runaway marriages, had been demolished in the 1870s to make way for the development of Knightsbridge. Its erstwhile Vicar, the Rev. H. B. Coward, urged its replacement with a church further west, and offered to donate the proceeds of the sale of the site of the Chapel towards its cost. From these beginnings came Holy Trinity in Prince Consort Road.

Its site was bought from the Commissioners for £6000 in 1901, the intention being to build 'a town church in the style and manner of the 14th century' to accommodate about 800 worshippers. Again, the designer was the great church architect, George Bodley then nearing the end of his career (he died in 1907). Due to its siting the building has a windowless east wall in anticipation of being overlooked by adjacent development, breaking with the tradition of an east end altar. It also now stands officially within Westminster, having been relinquished in 1901 boundary changes. Filled with interesting decoration this is considered to

146. The interior of Holy Trinity.

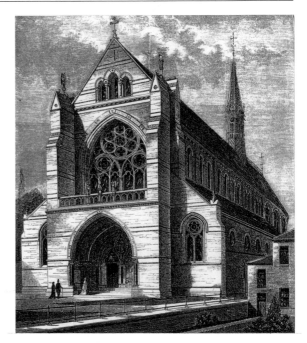

147. Our Lady of Victories, depicted in 1868.

be one of Bodley's finest buildings. The organ was moved there from the old Knightsbridge Chapel although re-cased and finally rebuilt in 1958.

THE CATHOLICS

In 1813 the first Roman Catholic chapel to be built in Kensington since the Reformation was established in Holland Street. Dedicated to St Mary, it was situated on land leased from William Phillimore by Richard Gillow, a member of a well-known north-country Catholic family, and James Kendall, a candlemaker. The first priest was a French émigré, Giles Veille.

After the Catholic Emancipation Act of 1829, a charity school was added and by 1850, with the re-establishment of the Catholic Hierarchy, St Mary's took the role of parish church. The parish priest at the time was Father James Foley. His congregation was growing and the Carmelites had established their church and priory only yards from his small chapel. This encouraged him to move his flock further south and at the same time serve others of his faith now coming to live in the area of Kensington High Street. In 1863 he bought a site near the corner of Earls Court Road for just over £5000 to build a church to be named Our Lady of Victories.

The Rev. Dr. Henry Manning, who had become Cardinal of Westminster in 1865, decided to elevate this church to the status of a Pro-Cathedral pending the construction of the great Roman Catholic Cathedral in Westminster. Although Foley's plot extended back nearly 300 feet and had a breadth of over seventy feet at the rear, its frontage was already occupied by shops and a pair of cottages as well as a school and its playground on part of the eastern side. This meant that its entrance from the High Street was barely 30 feet wide until 1935 when a Gothic arch was built between two shops to provide a more prepossessing entrance to the building, until then almost completely hidden by the surrounding property.

Its design, by George Goldie, was based on the Gothic style of 13th-century France and had a mixed reception. Some criticised its 'magnificence as a reproach to the poverty of many of the Established churches in this richest suburban parish' and William Morris's business manager Warrington Taylor, declared it to be 'the coarsest piece of vulgarity.'

In 1940 the church was destroyed by enemy action and for seventeen years the congregation had to worship in temporary surroundings. Firstly in the nearby Kensington (Odeon) Cinema, then at the Cavendish Furniture Showrooms in the High Street which was rented for a shilling a year, and finally at Kensington Chapel in Allen Street, lent to them by the Congregationalists. Trees twenty feet high were growing in the nave of the bombed church before rebuilding began to the designs of Sir Adrian Gilbert Scott. The new church was consecrated in 1959.

CONGREGATIONALISTS

In 1794, a group of a Congregationalists leased a site from William Phillimore on which to build a chapel. They were led by William Forsyth, the King's head gardener at Kensington Palace and St James's Palace, John Broadwood, the piano maker, James Gray, the Brompton nurseryman and a Mr James Mackintosh.

The chapel, on the corner of Hornton Street and Hornton Place, soon proved too small, despite being enlarged in 1845. A few years later a considerable proportion of its members took the bold decision to move north to create the grand new Horbury Chapel at Notting Hill Gate, now Kensington Temple.

Even then, the remaining congregation, at the height of Nonconformist evangelism among the shop keeping and trading classes, was still too large for the old chapel. In 1853 they moved south to Allen Street to build another chapel with a four-columned Corinthian façade. From its high central pulpit the Rev. C. Silvester Horne, who later became an MP, preached to large congregations who came long distances to hear him.

In 1940 a bomb destroyed the hall at the rear of the Kensington Chapel and the organ loft and the rest of the building were declared unsafe. The congregation continued their worship in company with the Presbyterians at the temporarily repaired St John's. It was 1952 before the damaged building could be fully repaired and it was then leased to the Roman Catholics of Our Lady of Victories until their bombed church was rebuilt in 1958. When the Chapel congregation returned, they were joined by the congregation of St John's (see below) under the umbrella of the United Reformed Church. Extensive renovations were carried out on the Kensington Chapel in the early 1990s.

The original chapel in Hornton Street was taken over by the Baptists in 1858 and was demolished in 1927. A small schoolhouse at its rear which was used by the British and Foreign Bible Society from 1835 had been demolished much earlier for the building of the Metropolitan Railway in 1865.

148. The little Wesleyan Chapel can be seen at the end of Clarence Place north of the High Street.

PRESBYTERIANS

St John's Presbyterian Church in Scarsdale Villas was opened in May 1863 although it was known at this time simply as Kensington Presbyterian Church, the later title dating from 1887. The building cost £6,000, but many were disappointed by a very plain interior, bare plaster walls, poor plain pews and a wooden floor, which gave it 'a sense of depression.' Its architect was an austere Scot, J. N. McCulloch, and over the years many changes were carried out to make it more attractive. In 1928 the congregation was united with that of the Emperors Gate Presbyterian Church which was closing. St John's was badly damaged during an air raid in September 1940 and for a time joined their neighbours at Kensington Chapel until that too suffered. As we have seen (above) both congregations moved back into their original homes for a short while until the creation of the United Reformed Church.

During its last independent years the Minister at St John's, the Rev. Marcus Spencer, presided over a remarkable experiment in religious drama at a time when the depiction of Christ by an actor was still highly controversial. This was *The Man Born to be King* by Dorothy L. Sayers, a play which later enjoyed tremendous success on radio.

Michael Flanders and Donald Swann, very popular entertainers in the 1950s and 1960s, gave some of their earliest shows to audiences of young people here. In 1952 a young organist, John Tavener, was appointed, whose name has become known far outside the music world since his work for the funeral of Diana, Princess of Wales; he has also done much to encourage the popularity of medieval liturgical singing. Tavener left St John's in 1973, his last festive occasion featuring a work for trumpet and organ. In 1975 St John's was sold to the Coptic Orthodox Church, St Mark's.

MISSION TO THE RICH

In the mid nineteenth century the Bayswater Circuit of the Methodist Conference resolved to 'plant chapels' in more respectable locations rather than in poor areas. One of these was the newly-developed Warwick Gardens area, where a church was built at the corner of Pembroke Gardens. This was in 1863 and a few years later a visiting Minister found the new church still in pristine condition 'everything, including the congregation, had a shiny new look as if newly-varnished.' However, it was sparsely used and it was closed in 1925 and demolished to make way for houses.

The growth of Nonconformism in the mid nineteenth century is illustrated by the proliferation of chapels established within short distances of

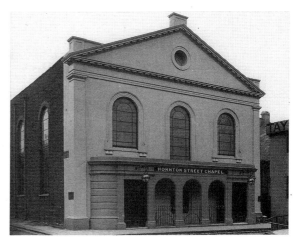

149. *Hornton Street Chapel.*

each other. Among these was the little Wesleyan Chapel in Clarence Place, in a side street to the north of the High Street, now Old Court Place. This was opened in 1862, and sat barely 200 people. It survived the late nineteenth-century redevelopment but later changed to secular use.

ARMENIANS

The smallest and surely one of the most beautiful churches in Kensington is St Sarkis, in Iverna Gardens, built in the 1920s through the gift of the millionaire Calouste Gulbenkian.

The small Armenian community in England had increased after the 1914-18 war and in May 1919 their spiritual leader, Dr Abel Abrahamian, made an appeal for funds to build a church in London. Insufficient money was raised, but the shipping magnate, Gulbenkian, agreed to provide £15,000 on the condition that it was dedicated to his parents, Mahtesi Sarkis and Dirouhi Gulbenkian, and designed in traditional Armenian style.

The model chosen was that of the little bell-tower of the St Haghpat Monastery, Armenia. At first the building held only fifty or so people but additions of a baptistry in 1937 and a sacristy in 1950 have provided a little more room. Although the interior is simple this only serves to highlight the little gem of a tiny chancel with its decorations of onyx, marble, alabaster and lapis lazuli with relief gilding designed by the Bromsgrove Guild.

When the Turkish invasion encouraged many Armenians to leave Cyprus and settle in England, little St Sarkis was unable to cope with their numbers and extra accommodation was taken at the redundant Church of England St Peter's in Cranley Gardens, South Kensington.

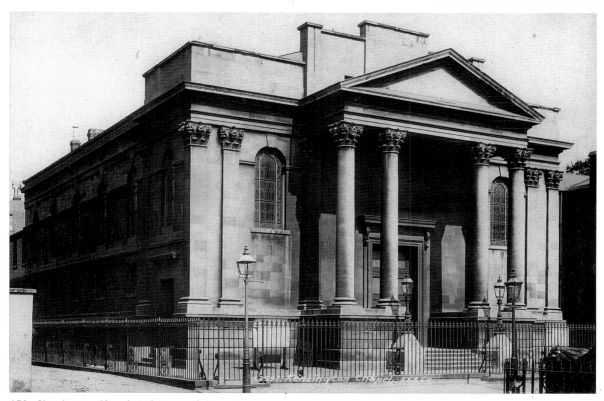

150. Kensington Chapel at the turn of the century.

EXILED RUSSIANS

In 1868 a Baptist Minister, the Rev. Stephen Bird, who had been connected with the chapel in Hornton Street, decided to build his own place of worship in Emperors Gate. It was a very short-lived venture and by 1871 the building was up for sale, the mortgagee adding a steeple to the structure to make it more attractive. It was bought by the English Presbyterians who remained there until 1929 when they joined their Scots counterparts at St John's, Scarsdale Villas. The Russian Orthodox Church in Exile then took the Church briefly, but it was converted into a Health Centre in 1995.

CHRISTIAN SCIENTISTS

In 1919 a temporary church was erected in Wrights Lane by the congregation of the Seventh Church of Christ Scientist, previously at Queens Gate Hall in Harrington Road, South Kensington. This was replaced in 1927 by a large building on land surplus to Iverna Court. In 1985 two thirds of this building was demolished to build a seven-storey office and flats block with the Christian Scientists keeping

the remainder. In more recent times this has become the First Church, amalgamating with the congregation from Sloane Street where the church site has been sold.

WHITE EAGLE LODGE

The studio and animal painting school of the artist W. Frank Calderon in St Mary Abbots Place has outwardly changed very little since it was built in 1910. But behind its arched entrance is a series of chapels, an art gallery, a large library, meeting room and book shop of a charitable religious trust founded over sixty years ago, known as White Eagle Lodge.

In the early 1930s, the Marylebone Spiritualist Association and the London Spiritual Mission in Pembridge Place, Bayswater, were drawing numbers of people to hear the psychic teaching of 'White Eagle', a Red Indian Chief, through the medium, Grace Cooke, known as 'Minesta' of the Brotherhood of the White Light. 'Minesta' and her husband Ivan, known as 'Brother Faithful', then

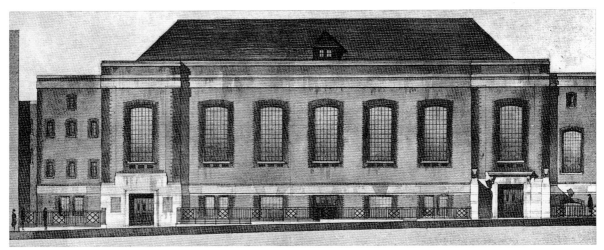

151. The design for the Seventh Church of Christ Scientist in Wrights Lane.

joined the Polaire Brotherhood in Paris, in which the family of Sir Arthur Conan Doyle had become interested. For a few years a centre was established at Burstow in Sussex, but when the lease of these premises expired in 1936 they moved to Pembroke Hall at the junction of Warwick Gardens and Pembroke Road, Kensington, where clairvoyance was combined with absent and contact spiritual healing.

The break with Paris came with the war and on 12 September 1940 a bomb destroyed Pembroke Hall but Grace and Ivan Cooke continued with their now considerable group of fellow members at 9 St Mary Abbots Place.

A monthly magazine was followed by a number of books and the opening of another Lodge in Edinburgh and in 1946, the acquisition of the next door house at St Mary Abbots Place where another chapel was set up. At the end of the war, the movement also had a big centre in Hampshire, known as New Lands, and in the decades since new Lodges have been established in many parts of Britain and abroad as well as a publishing trust. Today the activities include meditation and healing, the organisation of retreats and courses in subjects including yoga and astrology as well as regular services of worship and communion.

152. Grace and Ivan Cooke.

MORMONS

The American Church of Latter Day Saints (Mormons) erected a Temple in Exhibition Road in 1961 on the site of nos. 64/68 Princes Gate. The four-storey, spired building in re-inforced concrete and Portland stone incorporates a chapel, cultural hall, a children's section and a Family History Centre.

Old Schools

High up on the north front of St Mary Abbots School, facing the churchyard and Kensington Church Walk, are the painted stone figures of two children. The boy has a pen in his hand and a scroll inscribed 'I was naked and ye clothed me' and the girl holds a prayer book. The figures date from the early eighteenth century and used to stand outside the old parish school on the site of the former Town Hall in Kensington High Street.

This was not Kensington's first school for poor children. In 1654, Roger Peeble bequeathed two houses in the High Street as a free school. The Kensington Court Rolls note the renting of a room at the Catherine Wheel inn in Church Street, at sixpence a year, to house the schoolmaster. Children were taught reading and writing, particularly related to the scriptures, and occasionally arithmetic.

In 1705 Catherine Dicken and Mary Carnaby, left £90 to the parish school. The money was used in buying the Goat public house; when this was let out, five-eighths of the rent went towards the school's upkeep. In 1707 these and a number of other benefactions were merged and a subscription raised to fund a Charity School. Queen Anne subscribed £50 a year and her husband, Prince George of Denmark, added £30 to pay the schoolmaster's salary.

A Board of Trustees ran the school and subscribers were allowed to nominate pupils. On leaving the children were apprenticed or put into domestic service and sent out with a Bible and a copy *The Whole Duty of Man.*

The pupils wore a uniform, the boys in 'shutes with britches of blue leather, coats of warm kersey [thick woollen material], linen shirts, woollen hose and buckled shoes'; the girls had gowns of serge, blue aprons and 'quoiffs, riding hoods and pattens'. The boys also wore blue caps with crimson tosses (tassels) and crimson strings.

The Charity School was rebuilt in 1709 to the designs of Nicholas Hawksmoor, Clerk of Works to Christopher Wren at Kensington Palace. He did not charge a fee but forgot to contribute a promised £5 to the cost! It had a three-storey red brick frontage with a central bell tower. Although fairly commodious, by the early nineteenth century it was too small and in 1804 a new girls' school was built with a further extension, on the site of the old Coach & Horses pub, about ten years later.

153. One of the Charity Children figures, now on the front of St Mary Abbots School.

154. The Kensington Charity School shortly before its demolition.

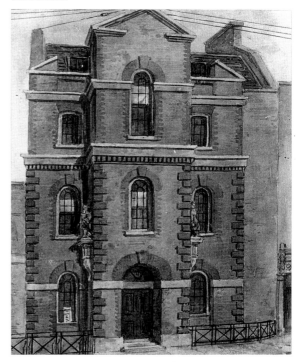

155. *A class at St Mary Abbots school c.1900.*

At about the same time it had become a 'National' school, administered by the educational body related to the Church of England. By the end of the century its premises had been enlarged even further to the rear into Church Court.

It was to this site that the whole institution moved in 1875 when the Hawksmoor building was demolished and its site used to build the new Vestry Hall. The two old stone figures of children were removed to the front of the new school.

Children of the poorer classes were also given tuition by the matron of Kensington Workhouse at Butts Field in the late eighteenth century, and at a Ragged School in the slum courtyards of Jennings Buildings (see pp. 136-137) in the 1850s.

Caroline Fox, the unmarried sister of the 3rd Baron, who settled at Little Holland House in the early years of the nineteenth century, founded a school for 'children of the labouring manufacturing and other poorer classes' on a site adjacent to her home in what became Holland Park Road. It survived long after her death in 1845 but with the advent of the London School Board in 1870 the building was considered unsatisfactory and the pupils were removed to a new school in Silver Street at the northern end of Church Street.

No Board Schools were established in the area after the passing of the Education Act of 1870, and only one of the new churches added a school to its facilities.

This school, at St Barnabas, was said to have been prompted by a newspaper report of a little girl crossing sweeper who, accused of having stolen two shillings, was sent to prison. The story so affected the Vicar of Kensington, Archdeacon Sinclair, that he decided to form a Boot Black Brigade to give children work and also to establish a school under the aegis of St Barnabas Church. A site was leased at 58 Earls Street (Earls Court Road) and from 1853 a gift of £10 a year towards its upkeep was made by the Duchess of Kent, mother of Queen Victoria. The Queen continued the subscription for forty years until her death in 1901. With the establishment of St Philip's in 1858 the two churches combined in the school's management and when it passed into partial control of the LCC in 1904 it remained Voluntary Aided. At the end of the century, numbers had grown enormously, a total of 559 pupils. When the lease came to an end, the site was bought by the parish at auction for £5000.

The school has continued to expand and always has a long waiting list. In the 1960s and 70s it was renowned for musical performances, several of which were broadcast.

The Nonconformist congregation at Hornton Street set up a school there until it was demolished for the construction of the Metropolitan Railway in 1868. A new school was built beside their Allen Street Chapel.

BOARDING SCHOOLS

The number of large houses in Kensington encouraged the establishment of private schools, particularly in the eighteenth and nineteenth centuries. Even earlier, Guy Memen, 'a doctor of physick' and a Huguenot refugee, ran a private boarding school for his own children and a few others at nos. 19 and 21 Young Street from 1694 to 1707. Scarsdale House was used as 'a boarding school of the first respectability' for young ladies, from 1755 to the 1840s.

In 1756, James Elphinstone, a well-known Scottish educationalist, took Kensington House to open an academy for boys. Leigh Hunt held the schoolmaster in high esteem and described him as a 'good old pedant.' Elphinstone was also a reformer of spelling and had ideas of introducing a phonetic alphabet. His many friends included Dr Johnson and Boswell who dined with him on Johnson's favourite dish of pork stuffed with plums.

Elphinstone left in 1776 and after some years of private occupation the house was taken by a French Jesuit, Victor de Broglio, as a school for the children of French émigrés, the young King Louis Philippe serving for a time as one of the ushers. Other pupils were the sons of West Indian planters sent to learn English.

A description of this academy is included in the memoirs of Richard Lalor Sheil, the Irish politician and dramatist, who was a pupil there in 1802-4. He writes of the principal, de Broglio, as 'a slender, gracefully constructed man, well-powdered and pomatumed, wearing a silk waistcoat and black stockings, his shoes with silver buckles giving him a glossy aspect.'

Sheil's fellow pupils were not so smart. He was seated next to the son of a French nobleman, 'a huge, lubberly fellow with thick matted hair which he never combed.' The sons of the West Indian planters 'were less attractive, though vain, foppish, generous and passionate.' Both sets of boys had one characteristic in common – they all detested England and greeted every French victory during the Napoleonic war with boisterous enthusiasm. At the end of the wars the school lost its purpose, and in 1815 new lessees took the house as a Catholic boarding house.

One of the inmates was the actress and novelist, Elizabeth Inchbald, who spent her last two years there finding it 'genteel and cheerful' although complaining that 'the residents changed too often for perfect cordiality.'

The houses of Kensington Square lent themselves to use as schools. The most enduring of these and also the largest, no 27, was taken in 1833

156. Pupils and teacher at Kensington Grammar School, 1880.

157. A certificate for French, given at Scarsdale House School in 1825.

by the Kensington Proprietary Grammar School to enlarge the institution, which had been established two years earlier at no 31. There was a cricket pitch and a playground in the large garden at the rear and a covered yard. The pupils spent at least a third of their time studying Greek and Latin and the teaching was by a monitorial system, older boys, instructed by the teachers, passing on their knowledge to the juniors. This was soon abandoned in favour of six classes and the subjects were extended. In 1841, the curriculum prepared boys for entry to the East India Company's colleges at Haileybury and Addiscombe with subjects such as Hindustani, military drawing, fortification, drill and fencing. The school flourished and expand with the acquisition of adjoining houses nos. 25, 26, 28 and 29, but a downward trend began in the 1860s when the railway cut off a large portion of the extensive playing area.

By 1869 the roll had dropped from its peak of 85 boys to only 45 and the directors voted to close it down as debts began to mount. At this point one of the Assistant Masters, the Rev. Charles Tabor Ackland, decided to make an offer to take it over. His newly named Kensington Foundation School opened in 1873 and for a time flourished until faced with the formidable rivalry of St Paul's

School at Hammersmith in 1884. By 1896 only ten pupils remained and the decision was taken to close the school and lease the front parts of the houses to private residents. Eventually all the school property was bought by the Crown and most of it leased to Derry & Toms to accommodate staff and for use as warehousing and workshops.

Peter Mark Roget who was to be the compiler of the famous *Thesaurus* was among the pupils of a school run by a Swiss, David Chauvet, at 42 Kensington Square from 1789-99.

The *Kensington Gazette*, between 1853 and 1855, offered a large choice of schools through its advertising columns, such as the English and French Grammar School at Stanford Villa, Stanford Road and Mr Povey's Classical and Commercial Preparatory School at Merton (Victoria) Road where 'the right directions of the noble sentiments and the excitement of mental activity are objects earnestly aimed at.'

A SCHOOL FOR SCANDAL

In 1873, Thomas John Capel (1836-1911), a well known and respected member of the Roman Catholic priesthood attached to the staff of the newly built Our Lady of Victories church, acquired Abingdon House near his home in Cedar Villa, off Wrights Lane, to establish a Roman Catholic University College. His venture had the full approval of the church's hierarchy, with whom Capel stood in high esteem for his skill in the conversion of Protestants, such as the 3rd Marquess of Bute. Critics described this sarcastically as 'perversion'.

Abingdon House was then altered for its new purpose to the designs of George Goldie, the architect of Our Lady of Victories. The conversion included an 'academical theatre', library, lecture rooms and a museum of specimens – although the curriculum stressed that science would be taught according to Catholic doctrine. A Senate was appointed as a governing body, whose members included the Duke of Norfolk. In October 1874 Cardinal Manning – whose Episcopal seat was Our Lady of Victories – performed a quiet opening ceremony.

The previous year, Capel had acquired a six-acre plot of railway land on the triangle between the lines near Warwick Road, Earls Court in order to open a Kensington Catholic Public School as a 'feeder' for the University College.

For a few years all seemed to be going well, the number of students at the College increased and Capel was able to enjoy his priestly status without sacrificing his 'love of good food, wine and every kind of luxury.' Disraeli based his character of

158. Schoolgirls playing cricket in the garden of the Convent of the Assumption in Kensington Square, c.1905.

Monsignor Catesby, in the novel *Lothair* on Capel.

The crash came in 1878 when Capel, deeply in debt not only for the University College but also his school at Earls Court, resigned. Later a publicly more serious reason than money troubles was disclosed. The priest had been named in connection with a homosexual clique in London.

He appealed to the Duke of Norfolk for help, while strenuously denying the accusations against him and pleading the sacrifices he had made for his academic ventures of 'family, social relations, finance and sleep.' Despite some gifts from sympathisers he still went bankrupt in 1880. The sale of his personal effects included thirty dozen bottles of wine. Both University College and school petered out and Capel left England for Italy, then America, where he died in 1911.

The Convent of the Assumption was established at nos. 23-24 Kensington Square in the 1850s – the nuns kept cows and chickens in the long gardens. Two schools were opened in one of the houses. These were followed by the building of a chapel, seriously damaged by fire in 1957, an elementary school in 1873 and a large secondary school and convent home for the nuns, in 1875-89. In the 1890s a finishing school known as St Catherine's was established at no. 20. The secondary school was evacuated during the Second World War and did not return and its place was taken by a teacher training school.

THE HIGH SCHOOL

In 1872 the first Girls' Public Day School Trust School was established in Chelsea under a headmistress called Miss Porter, at a salary of £250 a year out of which she had to pay her accommodation. A move to Kensington followed to what an early pupil, later Countess of Buxton, described as 'a hideous house' and then again to St Albans Grove in 1886, to Lytham House which had been built for the artist, Richard Ansdell. Here it remained until 1941 when the building was wrecked by a land mine. Apart from a brief period of evacuation the school remained in London throughout the war at Upper Phillimore Gardens.

After the war the accommodation was insufficient and it was decided to close the Senior school, but the Junior department continued under the GPDS Trust as the Kensington Preparatory School. Recently it has moved into the buildings of the Marist Convent in Fulham Road.

Past pupils of Kensington High School, as the senior school had been called, include Eleanor Rathbone MP, a pioneer in social services, Angela Thirkell, the novelist and Antonia Butler the cellist. The St Albans Grove building, when restored, became first the College of Estate Management and later part of the American Richmond College.

159. Market Court c.1865, one of Kensington's slum quarters.

Secret Slums

In mid-Victorian times Kensington had the air of prosperity. Shops proliferated along the gaslit High Street, large houses were being built in the new side streets, there was a prestigious new Vestry Hall and the great new parish church of St Mary Abbots was rising above its scaffolding. Yet, there was a down side, personified by the penny toy seller shivering in the gutter, or a weary, hollow-eyed labourer slipping quietly into a side alley on his way home from the brickyards to lodgings in one of the secret 'courts' only yards behind the bright shop fronts. Tucked away, between what is now the passage way to Kensington Court and Young Street, a slum of Dickensian squalor was a well-kept secret of 'the old court suburb' for over a century.

In Tudor times the Red Lion inn at the beginning of the High Street welcomed travellers as they entered the village from London. A large house with stables and outbuildings, Thomas Faulkner described it as 'much used by travellers', although in his day (the 1820s) it was no more. William Jennings, a saddler and harness maker, who built six small houses along its frontage, later converted into shops, had bought its courtyard in 1770s.

Behind them were two or more courts containing thirty or more cottages and soon other courts were added, the whole encompassed by the name of Jennings Buildings after its creator.

In 1841 Stephen Bird of the wealthy brickmaking and building family bought most of the area. Eight years later it was the centre of cholera outbreak, and Kensington Vestry was obliged to look seriously at its own ghetto rather than ignore it. The

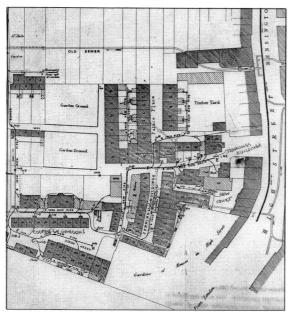

160. A map showing proposed new sewerage for the area of Jennings Buildings. The High Street is on the right.

Metropolitan Commission on Sewers disclosed that the alleyways were constructed on the line of a 'worse than useless sewer', only covered in places. A surveyor noted 'the crowded nature of the houses' but nothing was done, for despite its adjacency to the main Kensington street, once the cholera epidemic had passed, it was easy to ignore, because those who lived there – over a thousand people including a large proportion of children – had very little social contact with the rest of the community.

The men were mostly Irish labourers, at first working in the market gardens and later on building sites. The women also worked on the land, did washing, or were pedlars and hawkers. The majority of men lived as single lodgers, but where families lived together they occupied one room with no privy, drains or running water.

Jennings Buildings were described by the *Kensington Gazette* in February 1855 as 'truly horrible to conceive … in that narrow compass of that place are crammed nearly 1500 living souls, five hundred of whom are children'. It goes on to describe 'filthy and impassable lanes – where vice flourished and drunkenness rioted.'

The writer's concern was for the occupants' moral and spiritual welfare, noting that help was at hand…. A Sunday School was about to be established if £1200 could be found for a suitable meeting place. 'Before the mighty spirit of Chris-

tianity, Pestilence will retire and shrieks and moans change to the laughter of health and songs of joy.'

The Vestry opened a Ragged School in 1855 in Coopers Gardens, one of the constituent parts of Jennings Buildings, but nothing was done to remove the slum until 1873. Then, ironically, it was the profligate Baron Grant, anxious to enlarge the grounds of his new folly, Kensington House, who bribed the residents to leave by offering them £2 a room and any debris they wished to remove from their homes. Many of those displaced moved north to the notorious Potteries at Notting Dale, while the Baron obtained a semi-circular site to enhance his short-lived mansion.

Other working class enclaves existed behind the High Street in the eighteenth and nineteenth centuries but none so squalid as Jennings Buildings. These were situated on the Barker's site and dated from *c.*1707. One was named Halls Court after a bricklayer, Edmund Hall, and this extended to become Market Court and Gardeners Buildings, occupied mainly by market gardeners who were a poor but stable community.

On the north side of the High Street, Brown's Buildings, Clarence Place and other alleyways created a maze of little byways behind the shops on the south-east corner of Church Street. These were humble dwellings among which the old Royal Kent Theatre existed for a while (*see* pp. 145-146).

Those in work and without a skilled trade were very poorly paid. In the *Kensington News* in 1869 a postman wrote that he and his fellows were the hardest working but worst paid men, working from 7am in the morning to ten o'clock at night for fourteen shillings a week. The *News* advertised for 'a little girl for dressmaking – a small premium given weekly. Or, 'Wanted: Mangling – a penny a dozen. 'Wanted: a female servant for all duties including bread making, £8 a year.' The clergy of the parish ran a female servants' home where 'respectable female servants bringing a good character' could find lodging between jobs for 2s 6d a week.

In February 1869 the *News* noted that not all those who begged or received relief were destitute, nor was every parish officer 'a Bumble' as portrayed by writers such as Charles Dickens. It warned that another journal had taken up the case of the stone yard at the new workhouse, saying that it was 'ill-paid and its exposed position produced sickness and decay in those who worked there, apart from the noise of the breaking granite destroying the repose and embittered the dying hours of the aged and declining lodged nearby.' Whoever wrote that, said the newspaper, must be ignorant of human nature to wish to remove the incentive to honest hard work elsewhere.

The Patient Poor

In the nineteenth century the area between Marloes Road and the railway lines to its east became one of institutions. Here were built Kensington Workhouse and Westminster Workhouse, and also a Home for Crippled Boys.

Kensington Vestry built a small workhouse in the late eighteenth century on Butts Field, where Kensington Gate now stands. In 1846 this was replaced by a much larger building on eight acres called Broomfield, south of the High Street, approached only by an old lane called Barrows Walk. The site was 'situated on low and swampy ground through which passed a common sewer, with open ditches producing a most noxious effluvia'. Queen Victoria's personal physician remarked on being asked his opinion of the suitability of the site, that the Vestry's existing workhouse was situated on ground saturated with cesspools, with no sewer and no water laid on and little space for exercise. He thought the new site was perfectly suitable for the purpose.

The architect chosen for the new building was Thomas Allom. There were 'foul and itch' wards, separate lavatories for each class of inmate, workshops for stone breaking and oakum picking (untwisting fibre from old rope for use in caulking of ships), and chopping firewood.

Unusually, the workhouse building enhanced the location. It was built in 'Jacobethan' style, similar to the old Holland House, with a clock turret. Although cheaper white bricks were used in its construction, Allom faced it with red brick.

The building was joined quite soon to its south when the neighbouring parish of St Margaret's and St John's, Westminster, built a new workhouse outside of its own boundaries on the cheaper land of this part of Kensington. Here the architect was H.A. Hunt, whose design incorporated some humane and advanced features. Although the children were housed separately 'to protect them from contamination of evil habits and bad language', they did have a schoolhouse and a schoolmaster. There was also provision for 'married quarters' for elderly couples at a time when couples in workhouses were routinely separated.

The sanitary arrangements included running water and a ventilation system which in the winter the inmates preferred to do without as it relied very heavily on windows being opened. There were sixteen baths for 650 people, and there were 'refractory cells' for difficult inmates.

By 1870 this building was too small for the numbers housed there, and Westminster instead moved them to the newly built and much admired workhouse (later St Stephen's Hospital) in Fulham Road.

161. The Stone Hall at St Mary Abbots Workhouse, now incorporated into the new development.

162. St Mary Abbots Infirmary.

INFIRMARIES

Both these old workhouses near Marloes Road had small and primitive infirmaries. Here some trained nurses were employed but it was quite normal to use inmates who were either too old or too frail for labour in the workshops, or had 'a strong tendency to drink'. Doctors were part time, underpaid and supplied their own drugs as part of their fee.

In 1865 the deficiencies of workhouse infirmaries were taken up by *The Lancet*, which predicted that if they were improved they could become 'magnificent clinical hospitals instead of things of shreds and patches'. Louisa Twining, a pioneer of nursing training, had told a Committee on Poor Relief some years earlier that the supervision of nursing staff should be 'in the care of educated, responsible and conscientious women'.

In 1870 Alfred Williams, an up and coming architect (who was later to rebuild Harrods after the 1884 fire) designed a new infirmary at Kensington, plus an additional workhouse building. He chose the same style as his predecessor, Allom – 'Jacobethan'. In the 1880s particular measures were taken to exclude the childbirth killer, puerperal fever.

Before Westminster Workhouse moved to Fulham Road a plan to build a joint infirmary for the two workhouses at Kensington had come to nothing but once the Westminster building was empty the obvious solution to Kensington's problem was to use the Westminster Workhouse as an infirmary. In 1880 it was sold to Kensington for £55,000.

By the turn of the century the Infirmary was recognised as a 'general hospital' with specialist departments and when it was taken over by the London County Council in 1929 it became St Mary Abbots Hospital, though still incorporating institutional features such as a dormitory, day room and workshops for casual vagrants. It was not until 1938 that the word 'Institution' was dropped from the title.

After the advent of the National Health Service in 1948, the emphasis at the hospital was on psychiatry, geriatrics and the chronic sick, but in the 1980s with the building of the Chelsea and Westminster Hospital in Fulham Road, the old St Mary Abbots Hospital was sold and developed as housing and open space.

Two remnants of the old workhouse survive – the Grade I listed Stone Hall, and a drinking fountain in the external wall built in 1893 at the instigation of the Church of England Temperance Society. On it is the inscription:

Teach them true liberty
Make them from Strong Drink free
Let their homes happy be
God Bless the Poor

CRIPPLED APPRENTICES

Just to the north of Kensington Workhouse was the National Industrial Home for Crippled Boys, founded in 1869 in the old Woolsthorpe House off Wrights Lane. Here, crippled boys were taught the comparatively sedentary trades of printing and shoemaking.

The old house, one of three dating back to the days of Gregory Wright's development a hundred years earlier, had already been used as a school. Now, under the presidency of the Earl of Shaftesbury, it was converted to include workshops, schoolrooms, dormitories and an infirmary.

About sixty boys between the ages of 12 and 18 were taught stationery stamping, copperplate and lithographic printing, tailoring, carpentry, shoemaking and saddlery.

After the First World War there was a decline of entrants and in 1935 the site was sold and the proceeds, £37,500, used towards the building of the training college at the Royal National Orthopaedic Hospital at Stanmore. Kensington Close Hotel now occupies the site.

DISPENSING TO THE POOR

A Dispensary for the treatment of the sick poor was established in Holland Street in 1840 and this was moved to two houses, nos. 49-51 Church Street, in 1849. Shortly after, in 1855, the *Kensington Gazette* recommended Dr Ogier Ward, the dispensary surgeon, for the post of Medical Officer of Health. Dr Ward had recently published a report on cholera. In 1896 a ward was added to the Dispensary to accommodate eleven inpatients and its name changed to the Dispensary and Children's Hospital. By the 1920s it had vastly outgrown its premises and Princess Louise instigated the formation of a committee to establish a children's hospital. This materialised into the Princess Louise Hospital for Children in North Kensington in 1928.

163. Roselands Ward in St Mary Abbots Hospital, 1932.

164. David Wilkie.

Pens and Paint

Before the 'Leighton Settlement' around Melbury Road, Kensington's artists settled further east towards the Palace. Amongst these was Sir David Wilkie (1785-1841) a prolific painter of historical scenes who had at least three homes here.

The first, from 1813 to 1824, was at 24 Lower Phillimore Terrace, now the site of Safeway's supermarket in Kensington High Street, the second in The Terrace, between the present Wrights Lane and Adam and Eve Mews, and finally at Maitland House, now York House Place, from 1837-1841. It was during his residence at Phillimore Terrace that he painted one of his most famous works, *Chelsea Pensioners receiving the Gazette of the Battle of Waterloo,* commissioned by the Duke of Wellington in 1816 for which Wilkie was paid 1600 guineas counted in bank notes! The Duke visited his home to discuss the painting, with Wilkie's mother and sister watching his arrival from behind the net curtains in another room. After the Duke had left they decorated the chair he sat in with ribbons and recorded themselves as 'being quite put about for the rest of the day.'

THE MAGIC OF MILLAIS

When the Duke of Sussex presented the prizes at the Bloomsbury School of Art in 1839 the name of 'Mr Millais' was called out as the winner of the Royal Society of Arts Silver Medal and a small boy in a pinafore came forward to receive the award. It was the ten years old John Everett Millais. The following year he was admitted to the Royal Academy School where he continued to win prize after prize, culminating in the Gold Medal in 1847. The following year he became a founder member of the Pre-Raphaelite Brotherhood.

In 1855, Millais married Euphemia (Effie) the divorced wife of John Ruskin, although the two men remained good friends. Among others of his circle was William Thackeray at the time when he was in Palace Green and Millais had a house in Cromwell Place. Millais was so taken by his friend's new red brick house that in 1878, when it was his turn to house build, he chose no. 2 Palace Gate (*see* p.90)

During his long life, Millais' success never waned, the fame of his works making them public favourites far beyond the art world, such as *Bubbles* (the Pears soap poster), *Ophelia, The Vale of Rest, North West Passage* and, of course, numerous portraits. In 1885 he became a baronet and in 1896 succeeded Leighton as PRA, an office he held for

165. James Leigh Hunt.

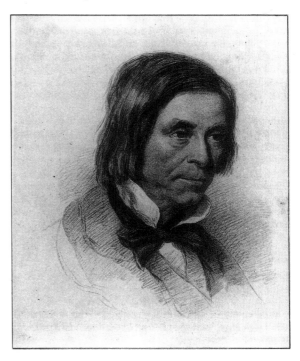

less than six months, as he died that year of cancer.

His successor was also a Kensington resident, Sir Edwin Poynter (1836-1919), who was to move into 70 Addison Road in 1905. Among his famous works are *Israel in Egypt* and the mosaic of St George in the Houses of Parliament.

LEIGH HUNT

Leigh Hunt (1784-1859) was not only a poet and journalist, but author of one of the earlier books on Kensington, *The Old Court Suburb*. This, written after Hunt had left Kensington, appeared originally as a series of vignettes for *Household Words* between 1853-55.

Hunt came to Kensington in 1840 when he, his feckless wife and numerous wild children, took 32 Edwardes Square. Here they stayed for eleven years before moving briefly to Phillimore Terrace, and then on to Hammersmith.

PAPERS AND PRINTERS

In 1852, Charles James Strutt, a jobbing printer with journalistic aspirations and a keen supporter of the Temperance Movement, published a local newspaper from his premises at the south end of Church Street opposite York House. His opinions did not prevent him accepting advertisements for brandy and gin at a shilling a pint but he offset this with lengthy editorial support for Nonconformist activities. He also fancied himself as a poet and rarely missed an opportunity to commemorate events in verse. *The Gazette*, at first a freesheet supported by its advertisers, later cost a penny but its life was short-lived, a mere two years.

It is generally supposed that James Wakeham, another printer, who founded the *Kensington News and West London Times* in 1869, was apprenticed to Strutt. Certainly it was 1854, just before Strutt left Kensington, that Wakeham set up his business at the northern end of Church Street.

In modern times the role of campaigning local journalist has been taken by the columnist, Harry James, of *The Kensington Times*, who in close co-operation with the local amenity and conservation societies, keeps an eye on developments, supported by his own extensive knowledge of the area. The latter is a rare quality in times when places of employment can be as transitory as places of residence.

Rachel Ferguson who lived in Kensington for most of her life, wrote three books on the area which did much more than chronicle its history during the first half of this century. They were *Passionate Kensington, The Royal Borough* and *We Were Amused*, the latter published after her death in 1957. In them she wrote of her personal impressions and associations with the well-known and colourful residents in that time, of which she was certainly one and without her many might have never been recorded.

THE RECORDING ARTISTS

Unlike Chelsea, which had James Hedderly, Kensington has not been blessed with an antiquarian photographer. Although the much-respected Dr John Merriman devoted much of his leisure time to photographing mid-Victorian Kensington Square and its environs, he was principally a busy physician, and Linley Sambourne was more interested in people than places. But there is a legacy from the professional photographers such as Argent Archer and H.R. Stiles, who had studios on the High Street and faithfully recorded changes in the area between the 1880s and 1930s. Several examples of their work are included in this book.

Therefore it is to artists that one must turn for some idea of street scenes of a century or more ago. Prominent among these is Thomas Hosmer Shepherd, whose brush and pencil complemented the words of the historians of the nineteenth cen-

166. *The masthead of the eleventh edition of* The Kensington Gazette, *15 February, 1854.*

tury, not only in Kensington but all over London. In 1923 Kensington Borough Council bought sections of a collection of Shepherd's works covering their area, which has provided an invaluable record.

In the last decades of Victoria's reign, a time of tremendous change, two artists took the last opportunity to record parts of London which might otherwise have been obliterated from memory.

William Luker (1867-1951), who signed his drawings W. Luker jnr., is a familiar signature beneath illustrations in books on old London popular at the time, and Kensington was among the areas in which he worked zealously. He is responsible for all the delicate line drawings in Loftie's *Kensington, Picturesque and Historical* published in 1888, the originals of which he gave to the Central Library.

Less known to the public were the watercolours by Elizabeth Gladstone (1858-1914), a doctor's daughter, who donated a marvellous collection of her pictures to Kensington Library in 1933. She married Henry Bach in 1896 and spent most of her married life in France, until her death in 1941.

Herbert Railton was an artist devoted to detail. He illustrated the 1902 edition of Leigh Hunt's *Old Court Suburb* edited by Austin Dobson, which one feels would have overjoyed the book's sad old author.

Frank Lewis Emanuel, the house artist of the *Manchester Guardian* for many years, was born in Bayswater in 1865, the son of an artist. He produced drawings of parts of Kensington the quality of which is equal to a photo lens with the added intimacy of an artist's eye. He lived in Ladbroke Grove for over twenty years and before his death in 1948 gave to the Borough over thirty of his topographical works.

In the 1930s once again two women were drawing Kensington. Joan Bloxam chose her subjects widely and her pictures of places such as South End are becoming historically valuable as the last vestiges of pre-war Kensington are gentrified. Gertrude Keeling is particularly well known for her studies of the Kensington Church Street area.

David Thomas could be described as a 20th-century Shepherd. A highly skilled draughtsman, he produced contemporary drawings for the *Kensington News* which are now historical records of the urban scene. Among the most valuable is a study of Holland House in its ruined state after the war, when he was granted special permission to enter the grounds. He also produced a number of large oil paintings of the City of London reminiscent of the works of Canaletto.

167. Ezra Pound.

REBEL POET

Kensington has usually been the home of the established artist rather than the avant garde. One exception was Ezra Pound (1885-1972). He lived at 10 Kensington Church Walk for five years from 1908 to 1913 and despite hating the church bells of St Mary Abbots he was married there in 1914 and declared that the area suited him very well. He had left America hoping that 'from London he could educate the educationable minority of the United States.'

He mixed with the elite of his day – Ford Madox Ford, Yeats, Epstein and Eliot – worked for journals such as *New Age* and *Poetry* and founded his Imagism poetic movement. Regarded as the pioneer of modern poetry and a militant pacifist, his social credit theories led him into Mussolini's Fascism and it was his broadcasts from Rome during the Second World War that led to his arrest and imprisonment in America in 1945. In 1946 he was adjudged insane and moved to an asylum where he remained until 1958. He died 1972.

168. *A band performance given by the Royal Horse Guards, in Kensington Gardens in 1856.*

Not Much Fun

For a comparatively well-to-do district, the town centre of Kensington was never very well served with places of entertainment other than public houses, perhaps because those who lived in its larger houses provided their own musical or dramatic events. These included, in much secrecy, the plays which Isabel, Lady Holland, the widow of the executed Earl, dared to enjoy at Holland House during Cromwell's protectorate. Although London theatres had been closed during the Civil War a few actors returned to London, risking imprisonment, and it was easier for them to take their productions to houses outside central London. One of these was Holland House where it is recorded they were seen by select gatherings of the nobility and gentry who used 'to make a sum for them, each giving a broadpiece [a gold coin worth just over a guinea] for the show.

Over a century later this venue again became the scene of theatricals, when participants included the lovely Lady Sarah Lennox (who very nearly became the consort of George III), the young Charles James Fox and Lady Susan Fox Strangways, daughter of Lord Ilchester. In 1761, when Lady Sarah was only sixteen, they presented *Jane*

Shore, which was seen by Horace Walpole who thought Lady Sarah 'more beautiful than you can conceive, all in white with her hair about her ears.'

The neighbouring mansion, Campden House, became renowned for its amateur theatricals in the mid 1850s when its occupant, William Frederick Wolley, built a 'perfect little theatre' there which was used by Charles Dickens and his company to present *The Lighthouse* by Wilkie Collins. This performance was in aid of the Sanatorium for Consumption and Diseases of the Chest at Bournemouth, a branch of the Hospital at Brompton. Dickens played the star role of the Lighthouse Keeper, the female roles being taken by Georgina Hogarth, his sister-in-law and his eldest daughter, Mary. Others in the cast included the artists Mark Lemon and Augustus Egg. Equally famous names were among the Moray Minstrels at Moray Lodge organised by the wealthy Arthur Lewis, of whom Dickens was also a member in company with William Thackeray, Arthur Sullivan, John Millais and George du Maurier. Lewis, founder of the Arts Club, became the grandfather of John Gielgud.

Such entertainment was, of course, enjoyed only by a few. There was then little public amusement, unless one counted the band performances which, according to the *Kensington Gazette* in August 1855, 'Her Majesty had given permission to be held in

Kensington Gardens on Sunday afternoons.'

Unfortunately the newspaper's joyful anticipation of the event was somewhat dampened by the quality of performance: 'A band of Life Guards performed in the most dreary manner the most dreary pieces of music that could be selected. It should be suggested to the Minister of Works, Sir Benjamin Hall that his good intentions would be better carried out by one of the German bands to be found every weekday in the West End.'

The standard of the playing was not the only complaint, some of those present, particularly the ladies, also protested about smoking in the audience. The Office of Works therefore decided to prohibit the practice in the vicinity.

BATTY'S HIPPODROME

A more exciting entertainment at about the same time was the famous Batty's Hippodrome, one of the 'side-shows' of the 1851 Exhibition, situated

to the south of Kensington Road between what is now Victoria Road and Palace Gate.

Established by William Batty, a circus proprietor, it was intended to attract the overflow crowds from the park, where Batty had originally hoped to establish it.

The Lady's Newspaper of 31 May 1851 wrote of 'the incredible feats of French equestriennes, probably the best horsewomen in the world', taking part in chariot races and two young Arabs riding ostriches – 'the birds have a marvellous speed and are trained admirably.' Brass bands played and other events included a monkeys' steeple chase. All this took place in an oval arena open to the sky, surrounded by eight rows of seats advertised to accommodate 14,000 people, although it is likely that the actual capacity was much less. There was also a riding school at the south end, which continued for about twenty years after the Hippodrome closed in 1852.

Kensington's only theatre closed after a very

169. *Dramatic happenings at Batty's Hippodrome in 1856.*

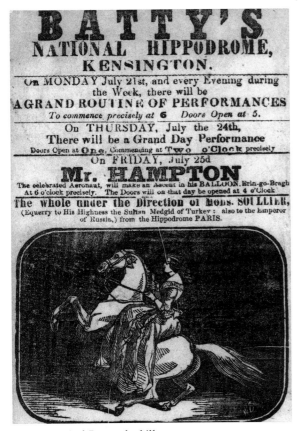

170. A typical Batty playbill.

171. The Royal Kent Theatre.

short and chequered career. This was the Royal Kent, situated in a narrow street off Kensington High Street known as Brown's Buildings – the site is now covered by Kensington Fire Station in Old Court Place. Known first as the Royal Kensington Theatre, the building was small, accommodating only about 300. The venture began as a subscription club theatre as it had been unable to get a public licence. When this was obtained through the support of the Duchess of Kent the name was changed in her honour.

The first production on 31 July 1831 was *Othello* and this was repeated when it reopened after a long closure in 1834. Productions during its seventeen years included classics such as *The Beggar's Opera* and *She Stoops to Conquer*.

The theatre usually opened at 6.30pm, the fashionable time in those days, but there was also admission for latecomers at reduced prices at 8.30pm The programme was arranged so that the audience saw at least one of the plays but many were drunk when they arrived anyway.

In 1838 there was a balloon ascent from the theatre's roof. But the Royal Kent was plagued with failures and disturbances including a riot, when being unpaid, the cast decamped after the first act one evening with the takings. The furious audience stormed the stage, broke up the seats and smashed the windows. When it reopened in 1841 the new manager was at pains to re-assure the public that he had no connection with the previous proprietor and that police constables would be present at every part of the house. In the end, the freeholder put the building up for auction but they failed to attract a buyer and finally, in 1849, it was demolished to build five houses.

SPEAKING SERIOUSLY

The editor of the *Kensington Gazette* in the 1850s, Charles Strutt, had no time for frivolous entertainment. He criticised Dickens in an 1855 editorial for an article in *Household Words* on Amusements for the People. Strutt declared that 'government and society should curb the licentiousness of pleasures and prevent them from degenerating into orgies rather than promoting them. People must be induced to seek their amusement in the direction of their duty and improving their worldly means, the care of their health and the culture of their minds, rather than attending games and gauds and raree shows.' The kind of events advertised in his *Gazette* doubtless met with his approval such as the talks given at the Kings Arms on *The Manners, Customs and Peculiarities of the Americans* or the *Structure of the Teeth in Men and Animals*. Admission to such events was a shilling – the same price as half a pint of gin.

Two Wars

'THE KENSINGTONS'

The shadow of events in Europe was not obvious from reading pages of the *Kensington News* in the hot summer of 1914. But from a world of horse shows, wrangles over the rates and suggestions to turn either the Broad Walk or Holland Walk into a traffic road, the local news moved into the urgent and exciting mood of a war that in its first days had almost a story-book unreality.

Queues of young men lined up outside the Town Hall to enlist in the Kensington Reserve Battalion, the 13th City of London Regiment, later known as Princess Louise's Own. Inside the building, classes were held 'for training ladies in the art of bandaging the poor wounded soldiers.' A Drumhead Service was held in Kensington Gardens, attended by Princess Louise and Princess Henry of Battenburg (Princess Beatrice), both of whom were living at Kensington Palace. On 21 August the 1st Battalion of Territorials, which only a few

172. A recruiting poster for Kitchener's Army.

LORD KITCHENER'S ARMY

KENSINGTON BATTALION

Appeal by His Worship the Mayor for the formation of a Kensington Battalion of the above Army.

The War Office are prepared to authorise the formation of a Kensington Battalion of Lord Kitchener's New Army for service until the end of the War provided 1,100 men can be recruited for such Battalion. The Terms of Service are as follows:—

Age on enlistment 19 to 35, Ex-Soldiers up to 45, and certain selected Ex-Non-Commissioned Officers up to 50. General service for the duration of the war. Height 5ft. 3in. and upwards. Chest 34in. at least. Medically fit. Pay at Army Rates. Married Men or Widowers with children will be accepted, and will draw Separation Allowance under Army Conditions.

Kensington has already shown its patriotism by enrolling in a few days to full strength, a second battalion of its local Territorial Regiment. I feel sure, however, there are still a number of men resident in or near the Borough who want to help their Country at this critical moment, and who will be willing to come forward and join the proposed Kensington Battalion.

I therefore make this earnest appeal to all who are eligible and willing to be trained for the defence of their Country to give me their names as being willing to present themselves for enrolment so that we may offer Lord Kitchener a Kensington Battalion.

I claim the co-operation of every loyal and patriotic citizen in the efforts which are being made to achieve this object.

Special arrangements will be made for men working together, or who know one another, to be enrolled in the same Company so that they may serve together.

Forms can be signed at the Town Hall, Kensington High Street, or at the Headquarters of the National Reserve, No. 102, Ladbroke Grove, Notting Hill, W.

Your King and Country Need You! Respond Quickly to the Call!

WILLIAM H. DAVISON,
Town Hall, Kensington, W. MAYOR.
September, 1914.

weeks before had been attending a training camp, left for France.

Recruiting immediately started for a 2nd Battalion which reached its full complement in three days, while women busied themselves with comforts 'for the boys out there.' 'A very welcome addition to the gift of socks is a small tin of boracic powder and a pair of leather bootlaces.'

This seemed almost to be playing at soldiers but within three months of the declaration of war the casualty lists began to come through. Among the first names was that of Prince Maurice, the youngest son of Princess Beatrice, who was killed in action on 30 October 1914, at the age of 23.

On 12 November, the Kensington Regiment began their march towards the front line in northern France, after an inspection by 82-year-old Lord Roberts of Kandahar, who collapsed and died two days later. At Christmas time, Princess Mary, only daughter of George V, later the Princess Royal, sent every man in the regiment a present of a briar pipe and chocolate. While the 3rd Battalion of recently enrolled Kensington recruits paraded at St Mary Abbots, the first deaths were reported from their comrades involved in savage fighting at Neuve Chappelle.

THE MAYOR'S BOYS

After the completion of the Kensington battalions there were still many young men clamouring to answer Kitchener's call to arms. The Mayor of Kensington, Alderman William Davison, offered to raise and equip another battalion, drawing on those still working in the area's shops and offices. At the same time volunteers from overseas, mainly from the Empire, were in a training camp at the White City. These were known as the 'Colonials' and formed A and B companies with Davison's

173. Kensington Red Cross Nurses.

174.   *Princess Louise inspecting the Kensington Battalion of the West London Volunteer Regiment.*

'Kensington's' as C and D companies of the 22nd Battalion of the Royal Fusiliers.

The Commanding Officer was Colonel Randle Barnett Barker, a remarkable man whose influence became legendary among those who fought under him. Over 200 'old soldiers' from the National Reserve provided added strength to this army of new soldiers.

The Mayor's responsibility extended far wider than mere recruitment. It included the provision of uniforms at a time when even khaki material was practically unobtainable. Help came from Harrods, who sent samples of serge and cloth and estimates for 2,000 uniforms at £1. 7s. 0d. each and 1,000 overcoats at £1. 5s. 6d. Derry & Toms supplied shirts and over a 1000 German-made Kropp razors to keep the men smart! Quartermastering did not end there. Davison also provided domestic necessities for nearly a thousand men, from bedsteads to knives and forks for the camp at Horsham,

which he also arranged. In July 1915, this largely citizens' army, now trained and fully equipped, was handed over to the War Office and by November 1915 was in France.

In the peaceful streets of Kensington, a War Supply depot was set up at nos. 10, 11 and 12 Kensington Square, where volunteers produced medical and surgical items. When visited in 1917 by the author E.V. Lucas, he was impressed by the ingenuity of the use of springs from newsprint rollers in the heads of crutches. This voluntary movement spread to other venues which were staffed almost entirely by women.

By the winter of 1915 the war was beginning to affect life at home. Food was getting short, although rationing was voluntary. At a Town Hall meeting the audience was told that as the poor had to eat more bread, the better off should avoid eating their full allowance and buy more expensive food!

TERRIBLE LOSSES

In July 1916, at Gommecourt, losses represented over half the Kensington battalions' strength. Further losses were incurred in September and October at the Somme and in 1917, at Arras, the third Battle of Ypres and Cambrai. Comrades often included the 22nd Fusiliers, who were also at Vimy Ridge and Passchendale. In May 1917, after the battle of Oppy Wood, Colonel Barnett Barker wrote to William Davison: 'My dear Willie, got safely out of the battle this morning. The regiment doesn't now exist ... only 40 men returned with me. They fought and died as heroes ... poor wounded lying out ... I am sick of bloody battles and everything connected with them. This murder of heroes is appalling...' On 6 January 1918 a special service was held at St Mary Abbots and the *Kensington News* wrote editorials headed 'Hold Fast' and 'Anxious Weeks.'

Though his practical support for the 22nd Fusiliers had ended in 1915, William Davison maintained a close personal relationship with its officers and men throughout the war, being informed of every casualty and writing to their next of kin.

At home there was the growing threat of air raids. Although the Zeppelin menace had been conquered there was a new danger from long range Gotha bombers. One bomb fell, with little damage, on the Central Library, then based in the old Vestry Hall. Air raid warnings were given by Special Constables and the regular police touring the streets on bicycles with bugles or sandwich-board notices saying 'Take Cover' and 'All Clear'.

The 2nd Battalion of the Princess Louise Regiment had gone to France but their main theatre of war was to be the Middle East, Salonika and Palestine, where they were heavily engaged but happily not decimated as their comrades had been in Flanders.

THE END

At the end of 1917, Barnett Barker, now promoted to the rank of General, was given the command of the 99th Infantry Brigade, and early in 1918 the 22nd Fusiliers, the old 'Colonials' and 'Kensingtons', were disbanded, the men being posted to other Fusiliers Battalions. In March 1918, General Barker was killed in action at Gueudencourt. An interesting postscript in peacetime was that Major Christopher Stone, who served with the Battalion throughout its life, became the first BBC 'disc jockey' with a programme of gramophone records during the 1930s.

In 1918, William Davison was elected Mayor for the fifth time and was knighted for his war services. He became MP for Kensington, South Division from 1918 to 1945 when he was elevated to the peerage and became Lord Broughshane.

When the Armistice was signed on 11 November 1918, flags flew, maroons were sounded and the 'bells of St Mary Abbots rang out a merry peal.' the *Kensington News* had the last word: 'we have had cause to rejoice ... the bullying Hun has been defeated and humiliated.'

Twenty-five years later, with the outbreak of the Second World War, the Princess Louise Kensington Regiment, which had remained as a Territorial Unit, was mobilised again, together with a great army of civilian volunteers which had been training since Munich and before. The Auxiliary Fire Service, Red Cross, Air Raid Warden and Rescue Services met at assembly points in the early days of September 1939 including the Barker's Depository in Pembroke Road, garages, schools and even private houses.

In the six years that followed the borough suffered over four hundred civilian deaths with nearly 3000 injured, as a result of over 12,600 bombs, both incendiary and explosive.

In the central area, around Kensington High

175. The bombed staircase of Holland House.

176. Members of the Wardens' Post 23 display gas masks, stirrup pumps, a pickaxe and a bicycle.

Street, one of the worst incidents occurred at St Mary Abbots Hospital when, on the night of 17 June 1944, a V1 Flying Bomb made a direct hit on the complex of buildings joined to the old workhouse. Five nurses, six children in the children's ward and seven adult patients died and 33 others were injured. The widespread damage, which included the RC Chapel, the domestic accommodation and part of the infirmary, closed the whole hospital, which was not fully restored until 1949. Earlier, in November 1941, another bomb had hit the hospital killing four people, including a ward Sister.

Enemy action had a severe affect on many of Kensington's old houses but most notable, of course, was Holland House. Other properties affected included the unique house, The Abbey (*see* p.100), which was completely destroyed. In Kensington Square, no. 36, the home of Lord Erne, who was killed at Dunkirk in 1940, was hit in the Blitz later that year. The house that had been built for the artist Colin Hunter at 14 Melbury Road in 1876 was among the studios destroyed, as was that originally occupied by the sculptor, James LeGrew, in 1845, and the artist Richard Ansdell in 1861 which had become part of Kensington High School in St Albans Grove.

In Lexham Gardens a terrace of six houses, Nos.45-53 were destroyed – Lexham House flats now stand there. The Museum and College area suffered much less, although one of the Norman Shaw houses in Queens Gate, no. 185, was destroyed. A V1 bomb fell at the corner of Vicarage Gate at lunchtime when the street was very busy with people, many of whom were killed or injured. It was also at lunchtime that heavy casualties occurred in an incident at the corner of Earls Court Road and the High Street, where four restaurants full of customers were badly damaged.

Despite rationing there was still some gratuitous food advice. Lord Woolton, the Food Minister, announced that 'powdered meat would soon be available.' *The Kensington News* told its readers how to make 'tasty morsels from bread' and 'how to get that new laid flavour with dried eggs.'

Vestry Hall to Town Hall

VESTRY AFFAIRS

In 1846 the building of a new workhouse in Marloes Road was the subject of bitter debate in Kensington Vestry. Indeed the treatment of the poor was generally contentious since most of them were in the slummier northern parts of the parish, beyond Holland Park Avenue, an area the wealthy ratepayers to the south rarely visited. Local government has always attracted tradesmen, a strata of society notoriously thrifty when it came to the levying of a parish rate: Between the wars it included Harold Kenyon of the undertaking firm,

Frederick Parsons, estate agent, Percy Barrs, chemist, Stanley Vandyk, photographer, a member of the Rawlings family (which invented the Rawlplug) and the builder Gordon Rawle. Another member was Henry Dickens, the grandson of Charles Dickens, whose views on building standards often brought him into conflict with Whitehall. There were also some titled people who lent their names and energy to good causes: Lord Balfour of Burleigh, founder of Kensington Housing Trust, Lady Petrie, later to become the Borough's first lady Mayor, and Lady Pepler. Each was involved in housing and public health.

The decision to build a new Town Hall came in 1875. The Vestry bought the site of the old Parish School, which had moved to a new building in Church Court, for £7,100 and two houses in Church Court. An architectural competition produced 65 entries but *The Architect* considered sixty of them

177. A children's party at the Town Hall c.1912.

to be 'of commonplace mediocrity.' A Gothic or Elizabethan design was excluded and the cost was to be limited to £18,000. An advisor was called in but the Vestrymen ignored his recommendation of a building in the fashionable Queen Anne style as 'looking like a Board School' and chose instead that by Robert Walker which the *Building News* considered to be 'commonplace Italian.'

The foundation stone was laid in 1878 and the building, which later served as Kensington Town Hall, was opened in 1880, its actual cost being over £30,000. It was described in *The Kensington Souvenir* in 1907, as 'solid and substantial rather than original and handsome.'

The old Vestry Hall was converted into a Central Library and opened by Princess Louise in November 1889, the Vestry having adopted the Public Libraries Act in 1887. The first free library had been established over ten years earlier by the philanthropist banker and MP, James Heywood, then living at Kensington Palace Gardens, at his own expense in Notting Hill Gate.

In 1871 the Board of Works had taken the site on the corner of Ball Street, behind Barker's, to build a fire station with accommodation for three married men, three single men, one driver, three horses and three engines. The station closed in 1912 when the present fire station was built in Old Court Place.

A police station had been opened in Church Court in 1830 on the right hand side of the archway, both being rebuilt in 1870. The station moved to new premises in Earls Court Road in 1956.

A LONDON BOROUGH

London's government was reorganised at the turn of this century and the London vestries disappeared, to be replaced by borough councils. Politically, Kensington Council has been dominated by councillors representing either ratepayers or the Conservative Party, but in the early 1930s the small Labour contingent from the North Kensington wards was growing in strength.

In the 1935 Parliamentary election, the 21-year-old Charles Hartwell challenged the popular sitting member for South Kensington, Sir William Davison, and had the young Clement Attlee supporting him. In the same election, Frank Carter, a taxi driver, who had been elected as a Labour councillor in 1928, stood against the Conservative, Captain J.A.L. Duncan, in North Kensington. He lost, but three decades later, in 1964, having served on the Council for over 35 years, he was made an Honorary Freeman of the Borough. Apart from his political experience, he also had a great interest in music and trees and was instrumental in the provision of a music room in the new public

178. Kensington Fire Brigade in the 1890s, outside the fire station in Ball Street.

179. Kensington's Jubilee Council meeting on 28 November, 1950. The presiding Mayor is Cllr John Gapp.

library. He served as an Alderman from 1945 to 1964 and after he retired continued his interests through the Kensington Society as a member of the Executive Committee. He died in 1991.

The early pioneers of Labour politics usually came from the trade unions – Walter Little, Henry Burns, Harry Bartlett, Arthur Byrd, and as women became more numerous in politics, Florence Smith, and Alice Jarrett were prominent councillors. Some of them were instrumental in a decision made in 1935 to stabilise the wages of its workmen with a sixpenny rise to bring the top class rate up to £3. 11s. 11d. a week. Frank Carter, together with Lord Balfour, Robert Jenkins and Henry Dickens were the last of the old Kensington Honorary Freemen before its amalgamation with Chelsea. In earlier years the honour had been conferred on Princess Louise in 1928, Winston Churchill in 1949 and Princess Alice in 1961.

A NEW COAT OF ARMS

In 1964, under the re-organisation of London boroughs, Kensington was united with Chelsea. This marked the end of the coats of arms of both local authorities, that of Kensington having been granted by the College of Arms in 1901, when Kensington became a Royal Borough. It was made up of the armorial bearings of those with historic associations with Kensington including the Abbey of Abingdon, the de Veres, Walter Cope, Henry Rich and Henry Fox. The motto was *Quid Nobis Ardui* – 'Nothing is too hard for us'.

The coat of arms for the new Borough is totally different, although the supporters of the shield, the Blue Boar and the Silver Winged Bull are a token representation of the de Veres and St Luke, the patron saint of Chelsea, and a bishop's mitre is included. The motto *Quam Bonum in Unum Habitare* is the Latin version of the opening words of the 133rd Psalm – 'What a good thing it is to dwell together in unity'.

Kensington Council's main post-war project had been the new Central Library on the old Abbey site in Hornton Street, designed by E. Vincent Harris and opened in July 1960 by Queen Elizabeth the Queen Mother despite considerable disruption caused by a demonstration against its design.

Soon after the amalgamation of Kensington with Chelsea, it was decided to replace Kensington and Chelsea Town Halls with a joint Civic Centre on the site of Niddry Lodge, the Red House and the remainder of the Abbey site. The architect of the new building was Sir Basil Spence. There was considerable dissent and a Public Enquiry was held before the foundations were laid in 1973.

180. Demolition of the Red House and Niddry Lodge, Hornton Street houses, to make way for the new Civic Centre.

Trees round the site were shored up during the digging of the foundations for the huge underground car park and Baroness Spencer Churchill planted a giant Redwood tree in memory of her husband. The new building was opened in 1977 and the next consideration was the future of the old Kensington Town Hall, now vacated.

BULLDOZED

As early as 1969 the GLC Surveyor of Historic Buildings had expressed the view that a Kensington Village Conservation Area should include not only Kensington Square and its environs but also the buildings on the north side of the High Street from the old Town Hall to the church. The Victorian Society was in favour of listing the Town Hall, the proposal being supported by the Kensington Society and many other local amenity groups.

The decision to sell the site for development provoked a public debate that went on for four years. Among the interested developers were County and District Properties whose proposal for the erection of a five-storey complex of shops and offices necessitated the demoliton of the old building. A condition of the contract, amounting to £5.4 million, was that planning permission was granted. The ensuing months saw letters of protest, packed public meetings and angry clashes with the Council's hierarchy.

Surprisingly perhaps, the Town Planning Committee refused planning permission to demolish the building. The developers appealed to the Minister and lost but taking advantage of this respite the opposition immediately took steps to have the building listed.

Then, on the morning of 11 June 1982, as darkness lifted, early risers discovered that almost the whole of the façade of the old Victorian Town Hall had been demolished during the night, only two days before a decision on a Conservation Order would have been made.

The mystery was soon solved. Two days earlier a letter from the Council was sent to County and District Properties saying that as agreed the previous day, 'there had been nothing in the Inspector's decision which said that the building was worthy of preservation. In these circumstances and to allow us to proceed to a redevelopment of the site at the earliest time, we consider immediate demolition to be advisable. Demolition works should be started on the evening of Friday 11 June that the maximum possible damage is done to the façade by continuous working over the weekend and that the work carries on until the whole site is cleared.'

A few days later, on 16 June 1982, another letter to the developers from the Council said that as a special meeting on the matter had been called by the GLC for Tuesday 22 June, 'it was critical that the back of the building was wrecked during the coming weekend.'

When these facts were made public a storm of protest broke out. The Kensington Society described the action as 'quite deplorable. For such tactics to have been used by an elected Council whose actions should be open and fully debated is quite shocking.'

The GLC placed a conservation order on what was left of the building but a bulldozer has a very final way of settling an argument. The building remained in its semi-demolished state while more plans were drawn up. These failed to get planning permission and went to appeal. Eventually the plan of a rival developer, by the architect Sir Frederick Gibberd, was approved for a modest three-storey shop and office complex and this went ahead in 1984.

LOOKING AHEAD

Arguments over other sites have taken place, such as Prince of Wales Terrace, the Warwick Road railway land, Kensington Barracks, St Mary Abbots Hospital, South End, Brompton Hospital and dozens of others. The framework for the Kensington of the future, as with every other part of London, is the Unitary Development Plan. A major feature of the UDP is the preservation and maintenance of the Borough's heritage by the establishment of Conservation Areas. Another matter of Council concern is the future of Kensington High Street and a firm of consultants has been commissioned to recommend proposals which would ensure its high standard as a shopping centre, control traffic, improve the streetscape and make it more pedestrian friendly.

An Environmental Awards Scheme was started in 1977 whereby annual awards are made to buildings too small for national award schemes, judged by a panel of independent assessors including the Council and amenity societies.

The abolition of the GLC changed the role of all London boroughs. Taking on some of the responsibilities of the GLC, such as education, Kensington now has a complex civil service structure. The intimate nature of local government is no longer possible and in its stead residents associations and amenity groups have proliferated. They play as large a part as the elected representatives they lobby in shaping the face of the neighbourhood. In such a way, the village, with its meetings in the Vestry at the side of the church lives on, although now there are many 'villages' and many rooms, and they run into each other with no fields in between. But the voices of the villagers are still heard.

181. The demolition of the old Town Hall in 1982.

Further Reading

The Survey of London, Vol. XXXVII *Northern Kensington* (1973)
  Vol. XXXVIII *Museums Area of South Kensington* (1975).
  Vol. XLVII *Southern Kensington: Kensington Square to Earls Court* (1986).
Bailey, Oliver and Mollier, Harold, *The Kensingtons* (1935).
Bowack, John, *Antiquities of Middlesex* (1705).
Brown, R.Weir, *Kenna's Kingdom: A Ramble through Kingly Kensington* (1881).
Cathcart Borer, Mary, *Two Villages* (1973).
Clunn, Harold, *The Face of London* (1932 rev. 1972).
Denny, Barbara, *Notting Hill and Holland Park Past* (1993).
Denny, Barbara and Starren, Carolyn, *Kensington and Chelsea in Old Photographs* (1996).
Duncan, Andrew, *Secret London* (1995).
Duncan, Andrew, Local history articles in *The Hill* (1986-1998).
Evans, Geoffrey, *Kensington* (1975).
Faulkner, Thomas, *History and Antiquities of Kensington* (1820).
Ferguson, Rachel, *Passionate Kensington* (1939).
Ferguson, Rachel, *Royal Borough* (1950).
Ferguson, Rachel, *We Were Amused* (1958).
Gaunt, William, *Kensington* (1975).
Gillett, Paula, *Victorian Painters' World* (1990).
Hudson, Derek, *Holland House in Kensington* (1967).
Hudson, Derek, *Kensington Palace* (1968).
Hunt, Leigh, *The Old Court Suburb* (1855).
Ilchester, The Earl of, *Home of the Hollands 1605-1820* (1937).
Ilchester, The Earl of, *Chronicles of Holland House* (1937).
Kensington News 1869-1972 (files)
Kensington News Centenary Supplement (1969).
Kensington Gazette 1853-1855.
Kensington Society Annual Reports 1954-1997.
Liechtenstein, Marie, *Holland House* (1875).
Loftie, Rev. W.J., *Kensington Picturesque and Historical* (1888).
Lysons, Rev. D., *The Environs of London* (1810).
Peel, D.W., *Garden in the Sky. Story of Barker's* (1960).
Ponsonby of Shulbrede, Lord, *Records of Kensington Square* (1987).
Ridgeway, Brigadier G.R., *Past Notabilities of Kensington* (1935).
Rosen and Zuckerman, *Mews of London* (1982).
Stone, Christopher, *History of the 22nd Battalion Royal Fusiliers* (1923).
Taylor, Pamela, Notes to Godfrey series of old Ordnance Survey Maps, Holland Park 1894 (1993), Kensington 1914 (1996).
Thackeray, Hester Fuller and Hammersley, Violet, *Thackeray's Daughter* (1951).
Walker, Annabel and Jackson, Peter, *Kensington and Chelsea* (1987).
Walkley, Giles, *Artists' Houses in London* (1994).

All of the above are held at Kensington Local Studies,
Central Library, Hornton Street, London W8 7RX.

INDEX
Illustrations are denoted by an asterisk